JOHN F. KENNEDY:

An Annotated Bibliography

by

Joan I. Newcomb

The Scarecrow Press, Inc.
Metuchen, N.J. & London
1977

Library of Congress Cataloging in Publication Data

Newcomb, Joan I
   John F. Kennedy : an annotated bibliography.

   Includes indexes.
   1. Kennedy, John Fitzgerald, Pres. U.S., 1917-1963
--Bibliography. 2. United States--Politics and government
--1961-1963--Bibliography.
Z8462.8.N48   [E842]   016.973922'092'4   77-7568
ISBN 0-8108-1042-5

CONTENTS

INTRODUCTION

In the brief span of years since the assassination of President John F. Kennedy in Dallas there has been a proliferation of literature dealing with his life and administration rivaling that of Franklin Delano Roosevelt and Abraham Lincoln. To date nearly seven hundred books have been published in the English language with President Kennedy or one of his family members as the subject.

It is the function of this bibliography to serve as a reference and a time-saver to scholars, students, librarians, collectors, and readers by bringing together in one source a comprehensive listing of these books.

Included in this listing are the bibliographic data for books published in the English language either in clothbound or paperback editions. References for paperback books are listed only if the book was not published previously in clothbound edition. Because the Kennedy literature is so voluminous, all books in a foreign language, and all pamphlets, and magazine, journal, and newspaper articles have been excluded.

The major sources of information in compiling this bibliography were footnotes and bibliographies from about 300 Kennedy books from the author's private collection, publications from the John F. Kennedy Library and the Library of Congress, and listings in several editions of Books in Print, Cumulative Book Index, and the Library of Congress National Union Catalogue.

Most of the references in the bibliography are annotated. These brief annotations serve to identify the general themes of the books or to provide information about the authors rather than present critiques or evaluations of the books.

The bibliography is arranged in nine major categories,

some with subheadings, and listed alphabetically by author. In cases where books fit reasonably into more than one category, cross-references are provided.

Part I of the book deals with the writings by John F. Kennedy.

Part II consists of biographies of John Kennedy and other family members and includes photographic collections and bibliographies.

Part III enumerates the books concerned with campaigns and elections.

Part IV refers to books on Kennedy's administration, whether of general, domestic, or foreign affairs content.

Part V of the bibliography covers books on the assassination.

Parts VI through IX compile books of tributes, poetry, fiction, and juvenile literature, respectively.

Grateful acknowledgment is made to Dr. Edward M. Silbert, associate professor of history at the University of South Florida for his encouragement and advice; to Jeanene McNair, librarian at the University of Southern Florida; to Mr. and Mrs. James Servies for providing me with bibliographic information from their private collection; and to Joy Fisher for sharing with me her collection of Kennedy literature.

Part I

WRITINGS BY JOHN F. KENNEDY

BOOKS

1 Kennedy, John F. , ed. As We Remember Joe. Cambridge, Mass. : University Press, 1945.
A 75-page collection of remembrances and tributes to his older brother, Joseph P. Kennedy, Jr. , who was killed in World War II. A private publication.

2 Kennedy, John F. The Burden and the Glory, edited by Allan Nevins. New York: Harper & Row, 1964.
A collection of speeches and public statements during the last two years of the President's administration.

3 Kennedy, John F. , et al. Creative America. New York: Published for the National Cultural Center, Ridge Press, 1964.
A depiction of artistic creation in America with photographs and text.

4 Kennedy, John F. , et al. Moral Crisis; The Case for Civil Rights. Minnesota: Gilbert Pub. Co. , 1964.
Statements by JFK and others on civil rights.

5 Kennedy, John F. A Nation of Immigrants. New York: Harper & Row, 1964.
A brief history of United States immigration. Originally published in 1958 as a 40-page pamphlet by the Anti-Defamation League of B'nai B'rith.

6 Kennedy, John F. Profiles in Courage. New York: Harper & Row, 1956.
A Pulitzer prize-winning book which describes acts of courage by eight former U.S. Senators.

7 Kennedy, John F. Sam Houston and the Senate. Austin, Tex. : Pemberton Press, 1970.

First published as chapter five of Profiles in Courage. Illustrated by Tom Lea.

8   Kennedy, John F.   The Strategy of Peace, edited by
    Allan Nevins.   New York: Harper & Row, 1960.
    A collection of the major speeches and public state-
    ments on foreign and domestic issues by JFK during
    his senatorial years.

9   Kennedy, John F.   To Turn the Tide, edited by John W.
    Gardner.   New York: Harper & Row, 1962.
    A selection of the major addresses and statements
    of the President during his first year in office.

10 Kennedy, John F.   Why England Slept.   New York:
    Funk, 1940.
    An expanded version of Kennedy's Harvard senior
    honors thesis which appraises England's lack of pre-
    paredness for World War II.

COLLECTIONS OF SPEECHES, STATEMENTS,
QUOTATIONS AND LETTERS

11 Adler, Bill, ed.   The Complete Kennedy Wit.   New York:
    The Third Press, 1966.
    Incorporates and enlarges upon material in previ-
    ous publications (see 13 and 14).

12 Adler, Bill, ed.   John F. Kennedy and the Young People
    of America.   New York: McKay, 1965.
    A collection of statements to and about young Amer-
    icans.

13 Adler, Bill, ed.   The Kennedy Wit.   New York: Gram-
    ercy Pub. Co., 1964.
    A collection of quips and humorous statements by
    the President.

14 Adler, Bill, ed.   More Kennedy Wit.   New York: Cita-
    del, 1965.

15 Adler, Bill, comp. and ed.   Presidential Wit.   New
    York: The Third Press, 1966.
    A collection of humorous statements by U. S. Presi-

dents. One chapter on President Kennedy with material taken from previously published books on Kennedy wit by the author.

16 Atkinson, Brooks, ed. College in a Yard: Minutes by Thirty-Nine Harvard Men. Cambridge, Mass.: Harvard University Press, 1957.
President Kennedy briefly recalls some of his Harvard days.

17 Barbarash, Ernest E. John F. Kennedy on Israel, Zionism and Jewish Issues. New York: Herzl, 1965.
Introductory notes by Gertrude Hirschler.

18 Chase, Harold W., and Lerman, Allen H. Kennedy and the Press. New York: Crowell, 1965.
A chronological presentation of Kennedy's press conferences, edited and annotated by the authors.

19 Country Beautiful Magazine, Editors of. America the Beautiful in the Words of John F. Kennedy. Elm Grove, Wis.: Country Beautiful Foundation, 1964.
An illustrated book of quotations from President Kennedy on "Man and the Land, Man and the Arts, and Man and His Dignity." Memorial statements by Lyndon B. Johnson, Stewart Udall, Richard Cardinal Cushing, and Allan Nevins.

20 Galloway, John, ed. The Kennedys and Vietnam. New York: Facts on File, 1971.
A collection of statements on the United States' involvement in Vietnam by President John F. Kennedy, Robert F. Kennedy, and Edward M. Kennedy.

21 Gardner, Gerald C., ed. The Quotable Mr. Kennedy. New York: Abelard-Schuman, 1962.
Quotations from JFK during his congressional and presidential years arranged in 12 topic headings.

22 Gardner, Gerald C., ed. The Shining Moments: The Words and Moods of John F. Kennedy. New York: Pocket Books, 1964.
Quotations from the presidential years of John F. Kennedy accompanied by photographs.

23 Goldman, Alex J., ed. The Quotable Kennedy. New York: Citadel, 1965.

A compilation of quotations from the writings, speeches, and press conferences of the President under approximately 75 topic headings.

Goldwin, Robert A., ed. Why Foreign Aid? (See item 426.)

24 Herndon, Booton. The Humor of JFK. Greenwich, Conn.: Fawcett, 1964.
A collection of witty remarks by President Kennedy.

25 Indian Book Co. Legacy of a President: The Memorable Words of John Fitzgerald Kennedy. Delhi: Indian Book Co., 1964.
A 108-page collection of quotations.

26 Jenkins, John H. Neither the Fanatics nor the Faint-Hearted: The Tour Leading to the President's Death and Two Speeches He Could Not Give. Austin, Tex.: Pemberton Press, 1963.
A slim book by a Texas author describing the presidential tour of Texas and presenting the texts of two planned addresses by President Kennedy.

27 Kennedy, John F. Address of President-Elect of the United States John F. Kennedy, Delivered to a Joint Convention of the Two Houses of the General Court of Massachusetts, January 9, 1961. Boston: Wright & Potter, 1961.
Also published as: An Address by John F. Kennedy, Delivered before the Massachusetts Legislature, January 9, 1961. Stamford, Conn.: Overbrook Press, 1961.

Kennedy, John F. The Burden and the Glory. (See item 2.)

28 Kennedy, John F. Every Citizen Holds Office. Washington, D.C.: Citizenship Committee, National Education Association, 1964.

29 Kennedy, John F. The First Book Edition of John F. Kennedy's Inaugural Address. New York: Watts, 1965.
Illustrated by Leonard Everett Fisher. Includes the Inaugural Address, L. B. Johnson's proclamation of a day of national mourning, and Robert Frost's poem, "The Gift Outright."

30 Kennedy, John F. Good Fences Make Good Neighbors.
    Convocation (Address) Oct. 8, 1957, the University of
    New Brunswick. Fredericton, N. B. : University of
    New Brunswick Press, 1960.

31 Kennedy, John F. Israel: A Miracle of Progress. An
    Address at the Golden Jubilee Banquet of B'nai Zion
    February 9, 1958. Washington, D. C. : U. S. Govern-
    ment Printing Office, 1958.

32 Kennedy, John F. Let the Lady Hold Up Her Head; Re-
    flections on American Immigration Policy. New York:
    American Jewish Committee, 1957.

    Kennedy, John F. , et al. Moral Crisis. (See item 4.)

33 Kennedy, John F. President Kennedy Speaks. Washing-
    ton, D. C. : United States Information Agency, 1961.

34 Kennedy, John F. President Kennedy's Program; Texts
    of All the President's Messages to Congress, Major
    Statements, Speeches and Letters in the First 100 Days.
    Washington, D. C. : Congressional Quarterly Service,
    1961.

35 Kennedy, John F. Quotations from the Scriptures. New
    York: Catholic Family Library, 1964.
        Excerpts from published speeches which contain
    quotations from the Bible. Includes the eulogy by Bish-
    op P. M. Hannon at the President's funeral.

36 Kennedy, John F. A Selection of Speeches and State-
    ments on the United Nations by President John F. Ken-
    nedy. New York: American Association for the United
    Nations, 1963.

    Kennedy, John F. A Strategy of Peace. (See item 8.)

    Kennedy, John F. To Turn the Tide. (See item 9.)

37 Klein, Arthur Luce, ed. Spoken Art Treasury of John
    F. Kennedy Addresses. New Rochelle, N. Y. : Spoken
    Arts, 1972.
        A 153-page illustrated book accompanying record-
    ings of addresses delivered by John Kennedy between
    1960 and 1963.

38   Lewis, Edward, and Rhodes, Richard.   John F. Kennedy:
     Words to Remember.   New York: Hallmark, 1967.

     Marshall, Robert A., ed.   Kennedy & Africa.   (See item
     451.)

39   Meyersohn, Maxwell, comp.   Memorable Quotations of
     John F. Kennedy.   New York: Crowell, 1965.
     Quotations from the President with subheadings un-
     der the major classifications of "The World in Crisis"
     and "The Affairs of the Nation."

40   O'Hara, William T., ed.   John F. Kennedy on Education.
     New York: Teachers' College, Columbia University
     Press, 1966.
     A selected and edited compilation of writings and
     statements on education by President Kennedy from his
     congressional and presidential years.

41   Peacock Press, Editors of.   A Kennedy Keepsake--John
     F. Kennedy, 1917-1963.   Berkeley, Calif.:   Peacock
     Press, 1964.
     Contains six quotations of President Kennedy.

42   Random House, Editors of.   A John F. Kennedy Memor-
     ial Miniature.   New York: Random House, 1966.
     An illustrated collection of a few of Kennedy's most
     noted quotations.

43   Schneider, the Rev. Nicholas A.   Religious Views of
     President John F. Kennedy in His Own Words.   St.
     Louis, Mo.:   Herder, 1965.
     Quotations excerpted primarily from addresses and
     public statements.

44   Schneider, the Rev. Nicholas A., and Rockhill, Nathalie
     S., comps. and eds.   John F. Kennedy Talks to Young
     People.   New York: Hawthorn, 1968.

45   Schwarz, Urs, ed.   John F. Kennedy, 1917-1963.   Lon-
     don: Hamlyn, 1964.
     A collection of addresses and essays by President
     Kennedy.

46   Settel, T. S., ed.   The Faith of JFK.   New York: Dut-
     ton, 1965.
     An anthology of biblical quotations, inspirational

poems, inspirational quotations and statements concerning faith, religion, and the church from the speeches and writings of President Kennedy.

47 United States. Congress. John Fitzgerald Kennedy: A Compilation of Statements and Speeches Made During His Service in the United States Senate and House of Representatives. Washington, D. C.: U. S. Government Printing Office, 1964.

48/9* United States. Congress. Senate. Committee on Commerce. Freedom of Communications: Final Report ... Pursuant to S. Res. 305, 86th Congress. Part I: The Speeches, Remarks, Press Conferences, and Statements of Senator John F. Kennedy, August 1 Through November 7, 1960. Washington, D. C.: U. S. Government Printing Office, 1961.

50 United States. Congress. Senate. Committee on Commerce. Freedom of Communications: Final Report ... Part III: The Joint Appearances of Senator John F. Kennedy and Vice President Richard M. Nixon and Other 1960 Campaign Presentations. Washington, D. C.: U. S. Government Printing Office, 1961.

51 United States. Congress. Senate. Committee on Commerce. Freedom of Communications. Report ... Pursuant to S. Res. 305, 86th Congress, Providing for a Study of the Uses of Government Licensed Media for the Dissemination of Political Opinions, News, and so forth. Washington, D. C.: U. S. Government Printing Office, 1961.
    Includes appearances of Kennedy and Nixon and other 1960 campaign presentations.

52 United States. President. Public Papers of the President of the United States: John F. Kennedy. Containing the Public Messages, Speeches, and Statements of the President, January 20 to December 31, 1961.

---

*In the interests of completeness, the following work should also be noted: U. S. Senate. Committee on Commerce. Freedom of Communications: Final Report ... Part II: The Speeches ... [etc.] of Vice President Richard M. Nixon, August 1 Through November 7, 1960 (Washington: U. S. Gov. Print. Off., 1961).

Washington, D. C. :   U. S. Government Printing Office, 1962.

53 United States.   President.   Public Papers of the Presi-
    dent of the United States: John F. Kennedy.   Contain-
    ing the Public Messages, Speeches, and Statements of
    the President, January 1 to December 31, 1962.   Wash-
    ington, D. C. :   U. S. Government Printing Office, 1963.

54 United States.   President.   Public Papers of the Presi-
    dent of the United States: John F. Kennedy.   Contain-
    ing the Public Messages, Speeches, and Statements of
    the President, January 1 to November 22, 1963.   Wash-
    ington, D. C. :   U. S. Government Printing Office, 1964.

55 Waldron, James R.   8818.   Elizabeth, N. J. : Pageant,
    1965.
        A large portion of the book contains correspondence
    between the author and JFK.

56 Wszelaki, Jan H. , ed.   John F. Kennedy and Poland;
    Selections of Documents, 1948-1963.   New York: Polish
    Institute of Arts and Sciences in America, 1964.

Part II

GENERAL BIOGRAPHY

BOOKS

57 Adler, Bill, comp. Kids' Letters to President Kennedy.
New York: Morrow, 1962.

58 Associated Press. Triumph and Tragedy: The Story of
the Kennedys. New York: Morrow, 1968.
A well-condensed family biography depicting four
generations of Kennedys. Illustrated.

59 Barnes, Clare. John F. Kennedy: Scrimshaw Collector.
Boston: Little, Brown, 1964.
A history of scrimshaw with illustrations and text
on Kennedy's collection.

60 Bilainkin, George. Second Diary of a Diplomatic Correspondent. London: Sampson, Low, Marston, 1947.
An account of Europe in 1945 including John Kennedy's journalistic reporting of the elections in Great
Britain.

61 Bishop, Jim. A Day in the Life of President Kennedy.
New York: Random House, 1964.
Describes a "typical day" of the President. Based
on interviews with President and Mrs. Kennedy and
White House staff.

62 Blair, Joan, and Blair, Clay, Jr. The Search for
J. F. K. New York: Berkley, 1976.
A biography focused on a 12-year period, 1935 to
1947, depicting the physical, social-emotional, and in-
tellectual development from Kennedy's graduation from
Choate until the time he entered the House of Representatives. Based on primary source documents and
interviews with family, friends, and associates.

15

63 Bloncourt, Pauline. An Old and a Young Leader: Winston Churchill and John Kennedy. London: Faber, 1970.

64 Bradlee, Benjamin. Conversations with Kennedy. New York: Norton, 1975.
    Personal narrative by journalist and friend. Recounts many personal and political conversations with the President.

65 Brennan, John F. The Evolution of Everyman: Ancestral Lineage of John F. Kennedy. Dundalk, Rep. of Ireland: Dundalgan Press, 1968.
    Discusses the Kennedys and Fitzgeralds in Ireland.

66 Bryant, Traphes L., and Leighton, Frances. Dog Days at the White House: The Outrageous Memoirs of the Presidential Kennel-Keeper, Truman to Nixon. New York: Macmillan, 1975.
    A personal narrative including much backstairs gossip.

67 Burns, James MacGregor. John Kennedy: A Political Profile. New York: Harcourt, Brace, 1960.
    The first full-length political biography of JFK. Covers his congressional years.

68 Carr, William H. JFK: A Complete Biography, 1917-1963. New York: Lancer, 1964.
    First published in 1962 under the title, JFK: An Informal Biography.

69 Clinch, Nancy Gager. The Kennedy Neurosis: A Psychological Portrait of an American Dynasty. New York: Grosset & Dunlap, 1973.
    A psychohistorical interpretation of the Kennedy family with a negative appraisal of the President.

70 Cutler, John Henry. Cardinal Cushing of Boston. New York: Hawthorn, 1970.
    Contains two chapters on Kennedy family relationships with the Cardinal.

71 Dallas, Rita, and Ratcliffe, Jeanira. The Kennedy Case. New York: Putnam, 1973.
    A personal narrative on Kennedy family members by a former private nurse to Joseph P. Kennedy.

72 Damore, Leo. The Cape Cod Years of John Fitzgerald
    Kennedy. Englewood Cliffs, N. J. : Prentice-Hall,
    1967.
        A biography of the President's life at Hyannis Port
    from childhood to the presidential years.

73 Davidson, Bill. President Kennedy Selects Six Brave
    Presidents. New York: Harper & Row, 1962.
        Profiles of Presidents Washington, J. Q. Adams,
    Lincoln, A. Johnson, Arthur, and T. Roosevelt based
    on interviews with Salinger, Sorensen, and President
    Kennedy.

74 Dineen, Joseph. The Kennedy Family. Boston: Little,
    Brown, 1959.
        A general family biography by a Boston journalist.

75 Dollen, Charles. John F. Kennedy, American. Boston:
    St. Paul Editions, 1965.
        A biography from boyhood through the presidency,
    emphasizing the positive personal characteristics of
    President Kennedy.

76 Donovan, Robert J. PT-109: John F. Kennedy in World
    War II. New York: McGraw-Hill, 1961.
        A full account of President Kennedy's Navy years.

77 Dunleavy, Stephen, and Brennan, Peter. Those Wild,
    Wild Kennedy Boys! New York: Pinnacle Books, 1976.
        An account of the alleged amorous affairs of John,
    Robert, and Edward Kennedy written by two newspaper
    reporters.

78 Faith, Samuel J. See Jack Run. Newark, N. J. : Deane-
    bra Co. , 1963.
        Illustrated by Bob Lev.

79 Fanta, J. Julius. Sailing with President Kennedy; The
    White House Yachtsman. New York: Sea Lore, 1968.
        An account of President Kennedy's interest in the
    sea and boating, emphasizing activities during the presi-
    dential years.

80 Fay, Paul B. The Pleasure of His Company. New
    York: Harper & Row, 1966.
        Personal memories of JFK from his Navy days
    through the presidential years by a friend and confidante.

81 Hennessy, Maurice N. I'll Come Back in the Spring-
    time: John F. Kennedy and the Irish. New York:
    Ives Washington, 1966.
        An account of President Kennedy's Irish ancestry,
    Irish political heritage, visits to Ireland, and the presi-
    dential trip in June 1963.

82 Hess, Stephen. America's Political Dynasties from
    Adams to Kennedy. Garden City, N. Y. : Doubleday,
    1966.
        Contains a brief biography of the Kennedy family
    and its political involvement.

83 Hirsch, Phil, and Hymoff, Edward. The Kennedy Cour-
    age. New York: Pyramid, 1965.
        Chronicles acts of courage by President Kennedy
    and other family members.

84 Hirsch, Phil, ed. The Kennedy War Heroes. New York:
    Pyramid Books, 1960, 1961, 1962.
        An anthology of the World War II combat experi-
    ences of Kennedy, Freeman, O'Donnell, Gavin, Day,
    Joseph Kennedy, Jr. , Caplin, Lemnitzer, Salinger,
    Connally, Goldberg, McGovern, Dillon and Shoup.

    Kennedy, Rose. Times to Remember. (See item 273.)

85 Koch, Thilo. Fighters for a New World. New York:
    Putnam, 1969.
        A profile in photographs and text of the lives,
    ideals, and aspirations of JFK, RFK, and Martin Luth-
    er King, Jr. , by a German news commentator.

86 Lasky, Victor. J. F. K. : The Man and the Myth. New
    York: Macmillan, 1963.
        A negative appraisal of Kennedy's congressional
    and presidential policies and practices.

87 Lasky, Victor. John F. Kennedy; What's Behind the
    Image? Washington, D. C. : Free World Press, 1960.
        An appraisal of Kennedy as strong on style and
    short on substance.

88 Lawrence, Bill. Six Presidents, Too Many Wars. New
    York: Saturday Review Press, 1972.
        Personal and political remembrances by a former
    New York Times and ABC reporter and friend of Presi-
    dent Kennedy.

89 Lee, Bruce. Boy's Life of John F. Kennedy, rev. ed.
New York: Bold Face Books, 1964. (Dist. by Ster-
ling.)
Biography of the President emphasizing the early
years.

90 Lincoln, Evelyn. Kennedy & Johnson. New York: Holt,
Rinehart and Winston, 1968.
A personal narrative by JFK's personal secretary
on the relationship between President Kennedy and Vice
President Johnson.

91 Lincoln, Evelyn. My Twelve Years with John F. Kennedy. New York: McKay, 1965.
Personal narrative by Kennedy's secretary.

92 McCarthy, Joe. The Remarkable Kennedys. New York:
Dial, 1960.
A general family biography.

93 McClendon, Winzola. Don't Quote Me; Washington News-
women and the Power Society. New York: Dutton,
1970.
Memoirs of a White House correspondent. Includes
many references to President Kennedy and his press
conferences.

94 Manchester, William. Portrait of a President: John F.
Kennedy in Profile. Boston: Little, Brown, 1962.
A study of John Kennedy as President from April
1961 to April 1962 based on observations of and interviews with the President and forty friends, family, and
staff members.

95 Marvin, Richard. The Kennedy Curse. New York: Bel-
mont, n. d.
A chronicle of Kennedy family tragedies.

96 Miller, Alice P. , comp. A Kennedy Chronology. New
York: Birthdate Research, 1968.

97 Montgomery, Ruth. Hail to the Chiefs; My Life with
Six Presidents. New York: Coward-McCann, 1970.
Autobiography of a White House newswoman for the
New York Daily News. Contains six chapters on Presi-
dent Kennedy.

98   O'Brien, Lawrence F.   No Final Victories: A Life in
     Politics from John F. Kennedy to Watergate.   Garden
     City, N. Y. :   Doubleday, 1974.
     Autobiography of one of Kennedy's chief campaign
     strategists and the head of congressional liaison during
     his presidency.

99   O'Donnell, Kenneth P. ; Powers, David F. ; and Mc-
     Carthy, Joe.   "Johnny, We Hardly Knew Ye"; Mem-
     ories of John Fitzgerald Kennedy.   Boston: Little,
     Brown, 1970, 1972.
     Memoirs of O'Donnell and Powers describing their
     relationship with the President over fifteen years as
     companions, confidants, and White House staff mem-
     bers.

100 Paper, Lewis J.   The Promise and the Performance:
     The Leadership of John F. Kennedy.   New York:
     Crown, 1975.
     An analysis of Kennedy's concept of the presidency,
     methods of decision-making, role as public leader, and
     the presidential images and aftermath of his tenure.

101 Reston, James.   Sketches in the Sand.   New York:
     Knopf, 1967.
     A collection of writings from the New York Times
     by the author.   Includes a selection of more than 50
     articles on Kennedy ranging from 1958 to 1964.

102 Rosenberg, Hyman S.   Short, Short Biography of Presi-
     dent John F. Kennedy.   Newark, N. J. :   Alpco, 1963.
     A 15-page mini-paperback giving the highlights of
     President Kennedy's life and presidency.

103 Russell, G. Darrell, Jr.   Lincoln and Kennedy: Looked
     at Kindly Together.   New York: Carlton, 1973.
     Presents parallels in the lives, humor, faith, and
     assassinations of Presidents Lincoln and Kennedy.

104 Salinger, Pierre.   With Kennedy.   Garden City, N. Y. :
     Doubleday, 1966.
     Personal account by Kennedy's press secretary
     during JFK's campaign and administration.

105 Sanghvi, Ramesh.   John F. Kennedy; A Political Biogra-
     phy.   Bombay: Perennial Press, 1961.
     An account of Kennedy's congressional years.

106 Saudek, Robert. Associates, Inc. Eight Courageous
     Americans. New York: Bantam, 1965.
          Transcripts of the television series, "Profiles in
     Courage," inspired by President Kennedy's Pulitzer
     prize-winning book.

107 Schlesinger, Arthur M., Jr. A Thousand Days: John
     F. Kennedy in the White House. Boston: Houghton
     Mifflin, 1965.
          An account of the presidential years by the noted
     Harvard historian who served as special assistant to
     the President.

108 Schwab, Peter, and Sheidman, J. Lee. John F. Ken-
     nedy. New York: Twayne, 1974.
          A biography in Twayne's Great Thinker series.

109 Sciacca, Tony. Kennedy and His Women. New York:
     Manor Books, 1976.
          A report on the intimate trysts between President
     Kennedy and several women.

110 Sciacca, Tony. Who Killed Marilyn? New York: Man-
     or Books, 1976.
          Identifies federal agents as the murderers of Mari-
     lyn Monroe to cover up her affairs with John and
     Robert Kennedy.

111 Shannon, William V. The American Irish, rev. ed.
     New York: Macmillan, 1966.
          Includes a chapter on the White House years of
     President Kennedy.

112 Shaw, Maud. White House Nannie: My Years with
     Caroline and John Kennedy, Jr. New York: New
     American Library, 1966.

113 Sidey, Hugh. John F. Kennedy, President. New York:
     Atheneum, 1964.
          A portrait of the President and a chronicle of his
     presidency from the election to the assassination.
     Written by a White House correspondent for Time
     Magazine.

114 Slatzer, Robert F. The Curious Death of Marilyn Mon-
     roe. New York: Pinnacle Books, 1975.
          A book speculating on the relationship between

John and Robert Kennedy and Marilyn Monroe. Impli-
cates the Kennedys and federal agents in the cause of
her death.

115 Smith, Merriman. The Good New Days: A Not Entire-
ly Reverent Study of Native Habits and Customs in
Modern Washington. New York: Bobbs-Merrill, 1962.
An anecdotal and satirical account of the New
Frontier days by the dean of the White House press
corps.

116 Sorensen, Theodore C. Kennedy. New York: Harper
& Row, 1965.
A political biography from Kennedy's senatorial
years through his presidency by his special counsel
and major speech writer.

117 Sorensen, Theodore C. The Kennedy Legacy: A Peace-
ful Revolution for the Seventies. New York: Macmillan, 1969.
An evaluation of the political and ideological legacy of John and Robert Kennedy.

118 Steiner, Paul. 175 Little-Known Facts about JFK.
New York: Citadel, 1964.

119 Stuart, Friend. Of Kennedys & Kings. San Marcos,
Calif. : Dominion, 1971.

120 Thompson, Nelson. The Dark Side of Camelot. Chicago: Playboy Press, 1976.
A portrayal of the less positive qualities and the
amorous relationships of John, Robert, and Edward
Kennedy.

121 Travell, Janet. Office Hours: Day and Night. New
York: World Pub. , 1968.
Autobiography of Kennedy's White House physician.

122 Whipple, Chandler. Lt. John F. Kennedy--Expendable !
New York: Universal, 1962.
An account of Kennedy's Navy years as commander
of a PT boat.

Wicker, Tom. JFK and LBJ. (See item 399.)

123 Wicker, Tom. Kennedy without Tears: The Man be-

neath the Myth. New York: Morrow, 1964.
A brief essay portraying the human qualities of
President Kennedy. Authored by a White House re-
porter for the New York Times.

PHOTOGRAPHIC COLLECTIONS

124 Dobbins, James J. Dobbins' Diary of the New Frontier.
Boston: Humphries, 1964.
A collection of editorial cartoons by the author
depicting Kennedy from his congressional years to his
death.

125 Doud, Earl; Booker, Bob; and Foster, George. The
First Family Photo Album. New York: Rolton, 1963.
Captioned photographs accompanying the transcript
of "The First Family" record album.

126 Hamilton, Charles. The Robot That Helped to Make a
President: A Reconnaissance into the Mysteries of
John F. Kennedy's Signature. New York: Hamilton,
1965.
An illustrated description of President Kennedy's
use of a signature machine, secretarial signatures,
and the development of the President's handwriting.

127 Hoffman, James. First Family Album. New York:
MacFadden-Bartell, 1963.
A small photographic album of the presidential
family.

128 Hoopes, Roy. What the President Does All Day. New
York: Day, 1962. (Memorial edition reprinted in
1964 by Dell.)
A photographic presentation with brief text of a
typical day in the life of President Kennedy.

129 Life [Magazine], Editors of. John F. Kennedy Memorial Edition. Chicago: Time, 1963.
Biography depicted through photographs, text, and
quotations.

130 Lincoln, Anne H. The Kennedy White House Parties.
New York: Viking, 1967.

Describes and illustrates entertainment at the
White House.

131   Look [Magazine], Editors of.   Kennedy and His Family
in Pictures.   New York: Cowles, 1963.
Exclusive photographs from the files of Look.

132   Lowe, Jacques.   The Kennedy Years.   New York: Viking, 1964.   (Text prepared by the New York Times
staff under the direction of Harold Faber.)
A photographic biography of the President from
childhood to death.

133   Lowe, Jacques.   Portrait: The Emergence of John F.
Kennedy.   New York: McGraw-Hill, 1961.
A pictorial record of Kennedy from his childhood
to his inauguration, emphasizing his family and campaigns.

134   Lurvey, Diana, ed.   The Kennedys, America's Royal
Family.   New York: Ideal, 1962.
A 66-page photographic account of the first fam-
ily.

135   Meyers, John S. , ed.   John Fitzgerald Kennedy As We
Remember Him.   New York: Atheneum, 1965.
A compendium of photographs, essays, letters,
speeches, and quotations by and about the President
forming a unique biographical record.

136   Raymond, John, and Ballot, Paul.   The Thousand Days.
Island Park, N. Y. : Aspen Corp. , 1964.
A memorial account of the life and death of President Kennedy.   U. P. I. photographs are accompanied
by editorial commentary.

137   Saunders, Doris E. , ed.   The Kennedy Years and the
Negro.   Chicago: Johnson Pub. Co. , 1964.
A photographic account of President Kennedy's in-
volvement in civil rights.

138   Shaw, Mark.   The John F. Kennedys: A Family Album.
New York: Farrar, Straus, 1964.
Informal family photographs from 1959 to 1963.

139   Shepard, Tazewell.   John F. Kennedy: Man of the Sea.
New York: Morrow, 1965.

A personal narrative by Kennedy's naval aide
with more than 100 photographs.

140   Spina, Tony.   This Was the President.   New York:
      Barnes, 1964.
      Chiefly illustrations of the presidential years.

141   Stoughton, Cecil, and Clifton, Chester V.   Narrated by
      Hugh Sidey.   The Memories--JFK, 1961-1963.   New
      York: Norton, 1973.
      Photographs of Kennedy's home, family, and presi-
      dency by an official White House aide.

142   United Press International and Chase Studios.   John F.
      Kennedy, from Childhood to Martyrdom.   Washington,
      D. C. :   Tatler, 1963.
      Photographic biography.

143   Wolff, Perry S.   A Tour of the White House with Mrs.
      John F. Kennedy.   Garden City, N. Y. :   Doubleday,
      1962.
      A photographic account with television text and
      annotations based on the televised tour of the White
      House.

144   Wood, James Playsted, and Country Beautiful Magazine,
      Editors of.   The Life and Words of John F. Kennedy.
      Elm Grove, Wis. :   Country Beautiful Foundation, 1964.
      A brief biographical record of President Kennedy
      with photographs, quotations, and text.

145   Wortsman, Eugene, ed.   The New Frontier Joke Book.
      New York: MacFadden-Bartell, 1963.
      A collection of jokes about the New Frontier.
      Illustrated by Robert Weber.

BIBLIOGRAPHIES AND CATALOGUES

146   Committee to Investigate Assassinations.   American
      Political Assassination; A Bibliography of Works Pub-
      lished 1963-1970 Related to the Assassination of John
      F. Kennedy, Martin Luther King and Robert F. Ken-
      nedy.   Washington, D. C. :   Committee to Investigate
      Assassinations, 1973.

147 Crown, James Tracy. The Kennedy Literature: A
     Bibliographic Essay on John F. Kennedy. New York:
     New York University Press, 1968.
     Analytical essays on a selected bibliography of
     Kennedy works.

148 Dabney, Q. M., and Co. A Catalogue of Old, Used,
     Rare and Out-of-Print Books on John F. Kennedy.
     Washington, D. C.: Q. M. Dabney and Co., 1975.

149 Fensterwald, Bernard J., et al. Selective Bibliography
     on Assassination. Washington, D. C.: Committee to
     Investigate Assassinations, 1969.
     A mimeographed, eight-page bibliography of books
     on the assassination of American and world leaders.

150 John F. Kennedy Library. John F. Kennedy: A Read-
     ing List. Waltham, Mass.: John F. Kennedy Library,
     1974.
     A briefly annotated listing of books divided into
     three sections: writings of JFK, books about JFK,
     and books about the Kennedy administration.

151 John F. Kennedy Library. The Kennedys: A Reading
     List for Young People. Waltham, Mass.: John F.
     Kennedy Library, 1974.
     A listing of 48 books for children. Grade levels
     indicated.

152 John F. Kennedy Library. Robert F. Kennedy: A
     Reading List. Waltham, Mass.: John F. Kennedy
     Library, 1974.
     A selection of 11 writings by RFK and 35 books
     about him. Not annotated.

153 Minkus Publications, Inc. John F. Kennedy World Wide
     Memorial Stamp Album. New York: Minkus, 1964.
     Supplements issued annually.

154 Rochette, Edward C. The Medallic Portraits of John
     F. Kennedy. Mamaroneck, N. Y.: Krause, 1966.
     Catalogue of coins, medals, and tokens.

155 Sable, Martin Howard. A Bio-Bibliography of the Ken-
     nedy Family. Metuchen, N. J.: Scarecrow, 1969.
     A short list of books and articles, plus brief bio-
     graphical sketches of Kennedy family members.

156 Stone, Ralph A. , ed. John F. Kennedy, 1917-1963;
     Chronology-Documents-Bibliographical Aids. Dobbs
     Ferry, N. Y. : Oceana, 1971.
     A short listing of books and articles.

157 Thompson, William Clifton. A Bibliography of Litera-
     ture Relating to the Assassination of President John
     F. Kennedy. San Antonio, Tex. : Printed by Carle-
     ton Printing Co. , 1968. Rev. ed. with 1971 supple-
     ment printed by Jiffy Press (dist. by W. C. Thomp-
     son & Son).
     A listing of nearly 300 books and resource materi-
     als, including distributors and prices of some items.

158 United States. Library of Congress. John Fitzgerald
     Kennedy 1917-1963; A Chronological List of References.
     Washington, D. C. : U. S. Government Printing Office,
     1964.
     A selective listing of books and articles. A 25-
     page supplement covers 1964 publications.

159 United States. National Archives. Index of Basic
     Source Materials. Washington, D. C. : General Ser-
     vices Administration, 1970.
     Indexes 1555 Warren Commission documents ac-
     cording to: investigatory agent, agency preparing re-
     port, subject of report, and city where investigation
     originated.

160 Wenger, Kenneth R. John F. Kennedy: Memorial
     Stamp Issues of the World. Fort Lee, N. J. : 1970.
     Alphabetical listing by country.

161 Wrone, David R. The Assassination of John Fitzgerald
     Kennedy: An Annotated Bibliography. Madison, Wis. :
     State Historical Society of Wisconsin, 1973.
     Material divided into five classifications: biblio-
     graphic works, basic resources, articles, books, and
     miscellaneous (charts, maps, etc.)

FAMILY BIOGRAPHY

JACQUELINE BOUVIER KENNEDY ONASSIS

162 Associated Professional Services. A Salute to Jacque-

line Kennedy: The Bravest Woman in the World: The
Highlights and Shadows in Her Life from Inauguration
to Arlington. Los Angeles: Associated Professional
Services, 1963.
Chiefly photographs.

163 Bair, Marjorie, ed. Jacqueline Kennedy in the White
     House. New York: Paperback Library, 1963.
       A pictorial biography of Jacqueline Kennedy with
     an emphasis on the White House years.

164 Baldrige, Letitia. Of Diamonds & Diplomats. Boston:
     Houghton Mifflin, 1968.
       An autobiography in which the author, Mrs. Ken-
     nedy's White House social secretary, records her re-
     membrances of Kennedy family members, particularly
     the First Lady.

165 Bouvier, Jacqueline, and Bouvier, Lee. One Special
     Summer. New York: Delacorte, 1975.
       An illustrated account of the sisters' European
     visit in 1951, prepared originally as a gift to their
     mother. Illustrations and some original poetry by
     Jacqueline Kennedy and most text by Lee B. Radzi-
     will.

166 Curtis, Charlotte. First Lady. New York: Pyramid,
     1962.
       A biography during the first year and a half in
     the White House.

167 Davis, John H. The Bouviers: Portrait of an Amer-
     ican Family. New York: Farrar, Straus & Giroux,
     1969.
       A history of the Bouviers by a family member.

168 Galella, Ron. Jacqueline. New York: Sheed and
     Ward, 1974.
       A photographic record with text of Jacqueline Ken-
     nedy Onassis during the years of her marriage to
     Onassis.

169 Gallagher, Mary Barelli. My Life with Jacqueline Ken-
     nedy, edited by Frances Spatz Leighton. New York:
     McKay, 1969.
       A narrative by Mrs. Kennedy's personal secre-
     tary.

170 Hall, Gordon Langley, and Pinchot, Ann. Jacqueline
     Kennedy: A Biography. New York: New American
     Library, 1964.
          A general biography of the First Lady through the
     White House years.

171 Harding, Robert T., and Holmes, A. L. Jacqueline
     Kennedy: A Woman for the World. New York: En-
     cyclopedia Enterprises, 1966.
          A photographic biography with text which focuses
     primarily on the White House years.

172 Heller, Deane, and Heller, David. Jacqueline Kennedy:
     The Warmly Human Life Story of the Woman All
     Americans Have Taken to Their Heart, enl. ed.
     Derby, Conn.: Monarch, 1963.
          First published in 1961 as: Jacqueline Kennedy;
     The Complete Story of America's Glamorous First
     Lady.

173 Malkus, Alida S. The Story of Jacqueline Kennedy.
     New York: Grosset & Dunlap, 1967.
          A general biography.

174 Means, Marianne. The Woman in the White House;
     The Lives, Times and Influences of Twelve Notable
     First Ladies. New York: Random House, 1963.
          Biographical sketches illuminating the impact of
     12 first ladies, including Mrs. Kennedy. Gathered
     from presidential interviews and historical records.
     Written by a White House correspondent.

175 Pioneer Books. A Proposal to Jacqueline Kennedy.
     New York: Pioneer Books, 1966.
          A 128-page volume suggesting Mrs. Kennedy run
     for President of the United States.

176 Pollard, Eve. Jackie. London: MacDonald & Co.,
     1969.

177 Rhea, Mini, and Leighton, Frances Spatz. I Was Jac-
     queline Kennedy's Dressmaker. New York: Fleet,
     1962.
          Remembrances of Mrs. Rhea, a Washington dress-
     maker and designer.

178 Safran, Claire, ed. Jacqueline Kennedy, Woman of

Valor. New York: MacFadden-Bartell, 1964.
Primarily a photographic biography of Mrs. Kennedy, emphasizing her demeanor throughout the as-
assination and funeral of the President.

179 Shulman, Irving. "Jackie"! The Exploitation of a First
Lady. New York: Trident, 1970.
A study of the exploitation, particularly by fan
magazines, of Mrs. Kennedy from the time she entered the White House until her marriage to Onassis.

180 Sparks, Fred. The $20,000,000 Honeymoon: Jackie
and Ari's First Year. New York: Bernard Geis,
1970.
A chronicle of events and expenditures during the
first year of marriage.

181 Thayer, Mary Van Rensselaer. Jacqueline Bouvier Kennedy. Garden City, N.Y.: Doubleday, 1961.
A warm, personal biography from childhood to the
inauguration. Written from family records and interviews.

182 Thayer, Mary Van Rensselaer. Jacqueline Kennedy:
The White House Years. Boston: Little, Brown,
1967.
A comprehensive biography of the First Lady during the White House years based on interviews and
private memoranda.

183 Watney, Hedda Lyons. Jackie. New York: Leisure
Books, 1971.
A biographical account of Jacqueline Onassis from
childhood to the death of Onassis.

184 West, J. B. Upstairs at the White House: My Life
with the First Ladies. New York: Coward & Geoghe-
gan, 1973.
The Chief Usher of the White House records his
remembrances of Mrs. Kennedy.

Wolff, Perry. A Tour of the White House with Mrs.
John F. Kennedy. (See item 143.)

ROBERT F. KENNEDY

185 Adler, Bill, ed. Dear Senator Kennedy. New York:

Dodd, Mead, 1966.
A selection of touching and humorous letters writ-
ten to RFK during his tenure as U.S. Senator from
New York.

186   Adler, Bill, ed.   A New Day: Robert F. Kennedy.
New York: New American Library, 1968.
A selection of quotations from Kennedy's sena-
torial years and presidential campaign.

187   Adler, Bill, ed.   The Robert F. Kennedy Wit.   New
York: Berkley, 1968.
A collection of humorous statements from Robert
Kennedy's years as attorney general and presidential
candidate.

188   American Heritage, Editors of.   RFK: His Life and
Death.   New York: Dell, 1968.
A photographic and written record of the life of
Robert F. Kennedy. Narrative by Jay Jacobs with an
eyewitness account of the last 36 hours by Kristi N.
Witker.

Bennett, Arnold.   Jackie, Bobby & Manchester.   (See
item 560.)

Blumenthal, Sid, and Yazijian, Harvey, eds.   Government by Gunplay.   (See item 619.)

189   Brown, Stuart Gerry.   The Presidency on Trial:
Robert Kennedy's 1968 Campaign and Afterwards.
Honolulu: University of Hawaii Press, 1972.
An analysis of Kennedy's campaign as a prospect
for "presidential leadership" and his death as a re-
turn to "presidential politics" written by a professor
of American studies at the University of Hawaii.

Chapman, Gil, and Chapman, Ann.   Who's Listening
Now?   (See item 368.)

190   Chester, Lewis; Hodgson, Godfrey; and Page, Bruce.
An American Melodrama: The Presidential Campaign
of 1968.   New York: Viking, 1969.
A comprehensive analysis of the 1968 campaign
by three reporters for the London Sunday Times who
traveled with the candidates.

Corry, John.   The Manchester Affair.   (See item 564.)

191   Country Beautiful, Editors of. America the Beautiful
      in the Words of Robert F. Kennedy. New York: Put-
      nam in association with Country Beautiful Foundation,
      1968.
         Photographs and quotations on youth, peace and
      freedom, law and liberty, man and his destiny, the
      inner city, and the America to come.

192   DeToledano, Ralph. R. F. K. : The Man Who Would Be
      President. New York: Putnam, 1967.
         A full-scale biography and critical account of Ken-
      nedy's political career.

193   English, David, and the Staff of the London Daily Ex-
      press. Divided They Stand. Englewood Cliffs, N. J. :
      Prentice-Hall, 1969.
         A journalistic account of the 1968 presidential
      campaign.

194   Freed, Donald. The Killing of RFK. New York:
      Dell, 1975.
         A fictionalized version of Robert Kennedy's assas-
      sination.

195   Frost, David. The Presidential Debate, 1968: David
      Frost Talks with Vice President Hubert Humphrey and
      Others. New York: Stein & Day, 1968.
         Includes Frost's interview with candidate RFK.

196   Gardner, Gerald C. Robert Kennedy in New York.
      New York: Random House, 1965.
         A narrative on Kennedy's campaign for the United
      States Senate by a speechwriter for that campaign.

197   Gordon, Gary. Robert F. Kennedy, Assistant Presi-
      dent: The Dramatic Life Story of the Second Most
      Powerful Man in Washington. Derby, Conn. : Mon-
      arch, 1962.
         A biography emphasizing the powerful position of
      RFK as confidant and advisor to his brother, the
      President.

198   Guthman, Edwin. We Band of Brothers. New York:
      Harper & Row, 1971.
         A personal narrative by a friend and assistant
      to Robert Kennedy covering Kennedy's career primar-
      ily from 1961 to 1968.

199 Halberstam, David. The Unfinished Odyssey of Robert
     Kennedy. New York: Random House, 1968.
     A chronicle of the personal and political growth
     of Kennedy focusing mainly on the 1968 presidential
     campaign.

200 Hall, Sue G., comp. Bobby Kennedy Off-Guard. New
     York: Grosset & Dunlap, 1968.
     A collection of quotations arranged in nine subject
     categories.

201 Hall, Sue G., comp. and ed. The Spirit of Robert F.
     Kennedy. New York: Grosset & Dunlap, 1968.
     Previously published under the title: Bobby Ken-
     nedy Off-Guard.

202 Hall, Sue G., and the Staff of Quote. The Quotable
     Robert F. Kennedy. Anderson, S.C.: Droke House,
     distributed by Grosset & Dunlap, 1967.
     Quotations arranged alphabetically by subject.

     Hopkins, Thomas A., ed. Rights for Americans. (See
     item 380.)

203 Houghton, Robert A., with Taylor, Theodore. Special
     Unit Senator: The Investigation of the Assassination
     of Senator Robert F. Kennedy. New York: Random
     House, 1970.
     An account by the Los Angeles Chief of Detectives
     in charge of the investigation.

     Imlay, Robert. The Cool War. (See item 331.)

204 Jansen, Godfrey. Why Robert Kennedy Was Killed:
     The Story of Two Victims. New York: Third Press,
     1970.
     A biographical analysis of Sirhan as a nationalist
     Palestinian and Sirhan's perception of RFK as a pro-
     Zionist.

205 Kaiser, Robert B. "R.F.K. Must Die!" A History of
     the Robert Kennedy Assassination and Its Aftermath.
     New York: Dutton, 1970.
     A comprehensive analysis presented chronological-
     ly from the assassination to the end of Sirhan's trial.
     The author served as an investigator for the defense
     team and the book includes material from interviews
     with Sirhan.

206   Kennedy, Robert F.   The Enemy Within.   New York:
      Harper & Row, 1960.
          A report and analysis of the problems and abuses
      discovered by the U. S. Senate Select Committee on
      Improper Activities in the Labor or Management Field,
      chaired by Senator McClellan.   Robert Kennedy served
      as chief counsel for the Committee and Senator John
      F. Kennedy served as a member of the Committee.

207   Kennedy, Robert F.   Just Friends and Brave Enemies.
      New York: Harper & Row, 1962.
          Twelve essays based on exchanges between the
      Attorney General and students, businessmen, and la-
      bor leaders in Japan, Indonesia, and Berlin.

208   Kennedy, Robert F.   The Pursuit of Justice.   Edited by
      Theodore J. Lowi.   New York: Harper & Row, 1964.
          Contains 12 essays on major problems faced dur-
      ing Kennedy's tenure as attorney general.

      Kennedy, Robert F.   Thirteen Days.   (See item 498.)

209   Kennedy, Robert F.   To Seek a Newer World.   Garden
      City, N. Y. : Doubleday, 1967.
          A collection of essays dealing with youth, race,
      the Alliance for Progress, nuclear control, China,
      and Vietnam.

210   Kimball, Penn.   Bobby Kennedy and the New Politics.
      Englewood Cliffs, N. J. : Prentice-Hall, 1968.
          A journalist's assessment of Kennedy as a leader
      of new trends in American politics.

      Knight, Janet M. , ed.   Three Assassinations.   (See
      item 574.)

      Koch, Thilo.   Fighters for a New World.   (See item
      85.)

211   Laing, Margaret Irene.   The Next Kennedy.   New York:
      Coward-McCann, 1968.
          A psychological and political portrait by an English
      woman journalist based on interviews with family,
      friends, and associates and a campaign trip with Ken-
      nedy and his staff.

212   Lasky, Victor.   Robert F. Kennedy: The Myth and the

Man. New York: Trident, 1968.
A critical appraisal of Kennedy's political career.

McKinley, James. Assassination in America. (See
item 581.)

213 Mahood, H. R. , ed. Urban Politics and Problems: A
Reader. New York: Scribner's, 1969.
Includes an article by RFK entitled, "Crime in
the Cities: Improving the Administration of Justice. "

Marshall, Burke. Federalism and Civil Rights. (See
item 385.)

214 Mehdi, Mohammad T. Kennedy and Sirhan, Why?
New York: New World, 1968.
A brief book describing the political ideologies of
RFK and Sirhan. Foreword by Kahlil Gibran.

Navasky, Victor S. Kennedy Justice. (See item 387.)

215 Newfield, Jack. Robert Kennedy: A Memoir. New
York: Dutton, 1969.
A narrative analyzing Kennedy's personal and political development from the time of his brother's
assassination until his death in 1968.

216 Nicholas, William. The Bobby Kennedy Nobody Knows.
Greenwich, Conn. : Fawcett, 1967.
Biographical highlights of Robert Kennedy preced-
ing his candidacy for the presidency. Written by
Time reporters Nick Thimmesch and William Johnson.

217 Quirk, Lawrence J. Robert Francis Kennedy: The
Man and the Politician. Los Angeles: Holloway
House, 1968.
A general biography of RFK.

218 Ross, Douglas. Robert F. Kennedy: Apostle of Change.
New York: Trident, 1968.
A review of Kennedy's public record analyzed by
a former legislative aide which illustrates the political
growth of Senator Kennedy.

219 Salinger, Pierre, et al. , eds. "An Honorable Profes-
sion": A Tribute to Robert F. Kennedy. Garden City,
N. Y. : Doubleday, 1968.

A collection of tributes, eulogies, and letters, primarily by journalists and politicians.

220 Schapp, Dick. R. F. K. New York: New American Library, 1967.
A full-length photographic biography.

221 Schoor, Gene. Young Robert Kennedy. New York: McGraw-Hill, 1969.
A biography emphasizing childhood and early development.

222 Shannon, William V. The Heir Apparent: Robert Kennedy and the Struggle for Power. New York: Macmillan, 1967.
An analysis of the personal background and political development of RFK emphasizing events following the death of President Kennedy.

223 Sheridan, Walter. The Fall and Rise of Jimmy Hoffa. New York: Saturday Review Press, 1972.
Chronicles the pursuit of Hoffa by RFK as a Senate investigator and attorney general.

Sorensen, Theodore C. The Kennedy Legacy. (See item 117.)

224 Stein, Jean. American Journey: The Times of Robert Kennedy, edited by George Plimpton. New York: Harcourt, Brace, Jovanovich, 1970.
A biography presented in narrative form from interviews with people associated with Kennedy's life and those aboard or watching the funeral train.

225 Swinburne, Laurence. RFK: The Last Knight. New York: Pyramid Books, 1969.

226 Thimmesch, Nick, and Johnson, William. Robert Kennedy at 40. New York: Norton, 1965.
A biography of Robert Kennedy by two journalists from Time magazine emphasizing the period from John Kennedy's assassination to Robert Kennedy's beginnings as a Senator.

227 Thompson, Robert E. , and Myers, Hortense. Robert F. Kennedy: The Brother Within. New York: Macmillan, 1962.

A biography emphasizing RFK's role as advisor to President Kennedy and as attorney general. Contrasts the personalities of the two brothers.

228   United Press International and Cowles, editors of. Assassination: Robert F. Kennedy 1925-1968. New York: Cowles, 1968.
A photographic and narrative chronicle from June 4 to June 9, 1968.

229   United States. Congress. Memorial Services in the Congress of the United States and Tributes in Eulogy of Robert Francis Kennedy, Late a Senator from the State of New York. Washington, D.C.: U.S. Government Printing Office, 1968.

230   vanden Heuvel, William, and Gwirtzman, Milton. On His Own: Robert F. Kennedy, 1964-68. Garden City, N.Y.: Doubleday, 1970.
A detailed study from the time of the President's death until his own assassination in California. Written by two friends and political associates.

Van Gelder, Lawrence. The Untold Story. (See item 587.)

231   White, Theodore H. The Making of the President 1968. New York: Atheneum, 1969.
A major, descriptive account of the campaign and election by a noted American historian.

232   Witcover, Jules. 85 Days: The Last Campaign of Robert Kennedy. New York: Putnam, 1969.
A detailed journalistic account from the time RFK announced his presidential candidacy to his burial at Arlington.

233   Zeiger, Henry A. Robert F. Kennedy: A Biography. Des Moines, Iowa: Meredith, 1968.
A brief biography which chronicles the highlights of RFK's life and political career.

EDWARD M. KENNEDY

234   Burns, James MacGregor. Edward Kennedy and the Camelot Legacy. New York: Norton, 1976.

A comprehensive analysis of Kennedy's Senatorial career and presidential prospects. A positive appraisal by an American historian, biographer of JFK, and delegate to several Democratic national conventions.

235 Chayes, Abram and Wiesner, Jerome, eds. ABM: An Evaluation of the Decision to Deploy an Antiballistic Missile System. New York: Harper & Row, 1969.
A dispassionate, inclusive, and exhaustive review edited by Chayes of Harvard and Wiesner of M. I. T. Prepared at the request of Senator Kennedy.

236 David, Lester. Ted Kennedy: Triumphs and Tragedies. New York: Grosset & Dunlap, 1971.
A favorable personal and political biography.

237 Hersh, Burton. The Education of Edward Kennedy: A Family Biography. New York: Morrow, 1972.
A full-length biography emphasizing developmental influences.

238 Honan, William H. Ted Kennedy: Profile of a Survivor; Edward M. Kennedy after Bobby, after Chappaquiddick, and after Three Years of Nixon. New York: Quadrangle, 1972.
A personal and political biography of EMK during the time of his brothers' assassinations, his near-fatal airplane crash, the accident at Chappaquiddick, and his defeat as majority whip in the Senate. Written by an editor of the Sunday New York Times.

Imlay, Robert. The Cool War. (See item 331.)

239 Kennedy, Edward M. Decisions for a Decade: Policies and Programs for the 1970s. Garden City, N. Y. : Doubleday, 1968.
A collection of essays dealing with five domestic and four foreign policy issues.

240 Kennedy, Edward M. , ed. The Fruitful Bough. Halliday Lithograph Corp. , 1965.
A privately printed collection of remembrances and tributes honoring Joseph P. Kennedy, Sr.

241 Kennedy, Edward M. In Critical Condition: The Crisis in America's Health Care. New York: Simon and

Schuster, 1972.
Essays advocating a comprehensive "Health Security Act. " Senator Kennedy has served for several
years as chairman of the Senate Health Subcommittee.

242 Levin, Murray B. Kennedy and McCormack: Dynastic
Politics in Massachusetts. New York: Bobbs-Merrill,
1964.
A study of the struggle for the Democratic nomination for Senator between the heirs of two politically
powerful Massachusetts families.

243 Levin, Murray B. Kennedy Campaigning: The System
and Style As Practiced by Senator Edward Kennedy.
Boston: Beacon, 1966.
An analysis of campaigning methods and practices
in Kennedy's first Senatorial race.

244 Lippman, Theo, Jr. Senator Ted Kennedy: The Career behind the Image. New York: Norton, 1976.
A detailed study of the senatorial career, generally favorable to Kennedy. Views Kennedy as an
impressive Senator, party leader, national celebrity,
and potential president.

245 Olsen, Jack. The Bridge at Chappaquiddick. Boston:
Little, Brown, 1970.
A day-to-day chronicle written by a senior editor
at Time.

246 Reybold, Malcolm. The Inspector's Opinion: The Chap-
paquiddick Incident. New York: Saturday Review
Press, 1975.
Fiction based on the events at Chappaquiddick.

247 Rust, Zad. Teddy Bare: The Last of the Kennedy
Clan. Boston: Western Islands, 1971.
An ultra-critical account of the Chappaquiddick
accident in particular and the Kennedy family in general.

248 Sherrill, Robert. The Last Kennedy. New York:
Dial, 1976.
A book divided into three major chapters: the
shaping influence of Ted Kennedy's father and brothers, the Chappaquiddick incident, and his senatorial
career.

249 Towle, Gertrude. Teddy. New York: Vantage, 1975.

250 Zeiger, Henry A. Inquest! Ted Kennedy--Mary Jo
     Kopechne--Prosecution or Persecution? New York:
     Tower, 1970.
         Excerpts from the official testimony at the in-
     quest.

                    OTHER FAMILY MEMBERS

251 Adler, Bill. The Kennedy Kids. Chicago: Playboy
     Press, 1976.
         Discusses the family life of the John, Robert, and
     Edward Kennedy families. Brief sketches on Caroline,
     John Jr., Kathleen, Joe III, Bobby Jr., and Teddy,
     Jr.

252 Barbrook, Alec. God Save the Commonwealth: An
     Electoral History of Massachusetts. Boston: Uni-
     versity of Massachusetts Press, 1973.
         Contains one chapter on the Kennedys of Boston.

253 Birmingham, Stephen. Real Lace: America's Irish
     Rich. New York: Harper & Row, 1973.
         Includes one chapter and several references to the
     Kennedy family.

254 Buck, Pearl S. The Kennedy Women: A Personal Ap-
     praisal. New York: Cowles, 1971.
         Portraits of the Kennedy women by an American
     Pulitzer Prize-winning novelist.

255 Callanan, Martin. Records of Four Tipperary Septs:
     The O'Kennedys, O'Dwyers, O'Mulryans, O'Meaghers.
     Galway, Rep. of Ireland: O'Gorman, 1938.
         Data on the President's Irish lineage.

256 Cameron, Gail. Rose: A Biography of Rose Fitzgerald
     Kennedy. New York: Putnam, 1971.
         A general biography of the President's mother.

257 Carr, William H. Those Fabulous Kennedy Women.
     New York: Wisdom House, 1961.
         Brief biographical sketches of the women in Ken-
     nedy's family.

258 Considine, Bob. It's the Irish. Garden City, N.Y. :
     Doubleday, 1961.
         Contains one chapter on the Kennedys, particular-
     ly the President.

259 Curley, James Michael. I'd Do It Again. Englewood
     Cliffs, N.J. : Prentice-Hall, 1957.
         Autobiography of a Massachusetts politician with
     several references to three generations of Kennedys.

260 Curran, Robert. The Kennedy Women. New York:
     Lancer, 1964.
         Brief biographical portrayal of the President's
     mother, wife, daughter, sisters, and sisters-in-law.

261 Cutler, John Henry. "Honey Fitz" Three Steps to the
     White House: The Life and Times of John F. (Honey
     Fitz) Fitzgerald. New York: Bobbs-Merrill, 1962.
         A full-length biography of the President's mater-
     nal grandfather, a former mayor of Boston. Dis-
     cusses the relationship between grandfather and grand-
     son.

262 Daniel, Lois, ed. The World of the Kennedy Women:
     Profiles in Grace and Courage. Kansas City, Mo. :
     Hallmark, 1973.
         A 61-page book illustrated by Bernard Fuchs.

263 David, Lester. Ethel: The Story of Mrs. Robert F.
     Kennedy. New York: World, 1971.
         A general biography, emphasizing family life.

264 David, Lester. Joan: The Reluctant Kennedy. New
     York: Warner Paperback Library, 1975.
         A biography of Mrs. Edward M. Kennedy.

265 Dineen, Joseph F. The Kennedy Family. Boston:
     Little, Brown, 1959.
         The first full-length biography of the Kennedy
     family written by a Boston journalist.

266 Dunn, Irma. Those Kennedys. New York: Vantage,
     n. d.
         Biographical sketches on several Kennedy family
     members.

267 Faber, Doris. The Mothers of American Presidents.

New York: New American Library, 1968.
Contains one chapter on Rose Fitzgerald Kennedy
with an emphasis on the relationship with her son.

268   Friedman, Stanley. The Magnificent Kennedy Women.
Derby, Conn.: Monarch, 1964.
A warm appraisal in biographical sketch form of
the Kennedy women.

269   Gager, Nancy. Kennedy Wives, Kennedy Women. New
York: Dell, 1976.
Biographical sketches of the Kennedy women by
a psychohistorian with a woman's liberation point of
view.

270   Handlin, Oscar. Boston's Immigrants. Cambridge,
Mass.: Harvard University Press, 1941.
Includes sections on the Kennedy and Fitzgerald
families.

271   Kennedy, Joseph P. I'm for Roosevelt. New York:
Reynal & Hitchcock, 1936.
A campaign book supporting the candidacy of FDR.

272   Kennedy, Joseph P., and Landis, James M. The Sur-
render of King Leopold, with an Appendix Containing
the Keyes-Gort Correspondence. New York: 1950.
A 61-page analysis written by the President's
father, former ambassador to Great Britain, and
Landis, dean of the Harvard Law School.

273   Kennedy, Rose. Times to Remember. Garden City,
N. Y.: Doubleday, 1974.
Autobiography of President Kennedy's mother. To
date the only autobiography by a family member.

274   Koskoff, David E. Joseph P. Kennedy: A Life and
Times. Englewood Cliffs, N. J.: Prentice-Hall, 1974.
A full-length biography of President Kennedy's
father. Detailed research.

275   Liston, Robert A. Sargent Shriver: A Candid Portrait.
New York: Farrar, Straus, 1964.
A biography of President Kennedy's brother-in-
law. Includes sections on Shriver's service in the
1960 campaign and as the first director of the Peace
Corps.

276 Marvin, Susan. The Women around R. F. K. New York:
     Lancer, 1967.
       Biographical sketches on Ethel, Rose, Jacqueline,
     and Joan Kennedy; the Kennedy sisters: Eunice, Pat,
     Jean, Rosemary, and Kathleen; Nicole Alphand; and
     Lee Radziwill.

277 Ney, John. Palm Beach: The Place, The People, Its
     Pleasures and Palaces. Boston: Little, Brown, 1966.
       Includes a section on the Kennedy family in Palm
     Beach, Fla.

278 Olsen, Jack. Aphrodite: Desperate Mission. New
     York: Putnam, 1970.
       An account of the World War II mission which
     took the life of the President's brother, Joseph P.
     Kennedy, Jr.

279 Searls, Henry. The Lost Prince: Young Joe, the For-
     gotten Kennedy. New York: World, 1969.
       A biography of the President's older brother.

280 Varma, K. Martanda. The Kennedys of Boston. Bos-
     ton: Trivandrum, printed at the Press Ramses, 1964.
       Brief biographical review of the Kennedy family.

281 Whalen, Richard J. The Founding Father: The Story
     of Joseph P. Kennedy. New York: New American
     Library, 1964.
       A major biography of the President's father which
     depicts him as a man of power, wealth, and family
     ambition.

282 Whitehill, Walter Muir. Boston in the Age of John
     Fitzgerald Kennedy. Norman: University of Okla-
     homa Press, 1966.
       A descriptive analysis of the city's development
     and institutions views as a center of civilization by a
     Harvard faculty member. Several references to John
     Kennedy and other family members.

Part III

CAMPAIGNS AND ELECTIONS

283 Barrett, Patricia. Religious Liberty and the American Presidency: A Study in Church-State Relations. New York: Herder, 1963.
Discusses religion and the campaign of 1960, Catholicism and American democracy, and the trend toward a realistic pluralism.

284 Bruno, Jerry, and Greenfield, Jeff. The Advance Man. New York: Morrow, 1971.
A personal account by Kennedy's major advance man in the 1960 campaign. Describes the function and work of an advance man.

285 David, Paul T., ed. The Presidential Election and Transition 1960-1961. Washington, D.C.: Brookings Institution, 1961.
A series of studies dealing with the history of the 1960 campaign and election, and the subsequent adjustments in the executive branch, Congress, and the political parties.

286 Dawidowicz, Lucy S., and Goldstein, Leon J. Politics in a Pluralist Democracy: Studies of Voting in the 1960 Election. New York: Institute of Human Relations Press, 1963.
Examines voting patterns in the 1960 election.

287 Ernst, Harry W. The Primary that Made a President: West Virginia 1960. New York: McGraw-Hill, 1962.
A study conducted under the auspices of the Eagleton Institute.

Fuchs, Lawrence H. John F. Kennedy and American Catholicism. (See item 324.)

288 Havard, William G.; Heberle, Rudolph; and Howard,

45

Perry H. The Louisiana Elections of 1960. Baton
Rouge: Louisiana State University Press, 1963.
(Social Science Series, no. 9).

289 Inaugural Committee, 1961. The Inauguration of John
Fitzgerald Kennedy and Lyndon Baines Johnson, January 20, 1961. Washington, D.C.: Inaugural Committee, 1962.
A collection of articles and illustrations primarily
reproduced from newspapers.

290 Inaugural Committee, 1961. Official Program, Inaugu-
ral Ceremonies of John F. Kennedy, Thirty-Fifth Pres-
ident of the United States and Lyndon B. Johnson,
Thirty-Seventh Vice President of the United States.
Washington, D.C., January 20, 1961. Washington,
D.C.: Inaugural Committee, 1961.
A 63-page illustrated program of the official in-
augural events.

291 Kraus, Sidney, ed. The Great Debates: Background--
Perspective--Effects. Bloomington: Indiana University Press, 1962.
A collection of studies analyzing the importance
of the televised Kennedy-Nixon debates. Includes ver-
batim text, photographs, tables, graphs, charts, and
floor plans. Studies by academic, network, and political analysts.

292 Levy, Mary R., and Kramer, Michael S. The Ethnic
Factor: How America's Minorities Decide Elections.
New York: Simon and Schuster, 1972.
Contains analyses of the elections of Edward M.,
Robert F., and John F. Kennedy.

Lincoln, Evelyn. My Twelve Years with John F. Kennedy. (See item 91.)

293 Longley, Lawrence D., and Braun, Alan G. The Politics of Electoral College Reform. New Haven, Conn.:
Yale University Press, 1972.
The 1960 election serves as a case study for explaining the electoral college.

294 Martin, Ralph G. Ballots and Bandwagons. Chicago:
Rand McNally, 1964.
A review of five national political conventions, in-

cluding 1956 and JFK's near miss for the Vice Presidential nomination. Stresses personalities and party politicking.

295 Martin, Ralph G., and Plaut, Ed. Front Runner, Dark Horse. Garden City, N. Y.: Doubleday, 1960.
     An account of Democratic Senators John F. Kennedy, the front runner, and Stuart Symington, the dark horse, seeking the 1960 nomination.

296 Michener, James A. A Report of the County Chairman.
     New York: Random House, 1961.
     A personal narrative by the noted American author who served as chairman for Kennedy's campaign in Bucks County, Pennsylvania.

     O'Brien, Lawrence F. No Final Victories. (See item 98.)

     O'Donnell; Powers; and McCarthy. "Johnny, We Hardly Knew Ye." (See item 99.)

297 Pike, James A. A Roman Catholic in the White House.
     Garden City, N. Y.: Doubleday, 1959.
     A discussion of the political consequences of a Roman Catholic if he were elected President. Written by a bishop in the Episcopalian Church and published shortly before the 1960 election.

298 Pool, Ithiel deSola; Abelson, Robert P.; and Popkin, Samuel. Candidates, Issues, and Strategies: A Computer Simulation of the 1960 Presidential Election.
     Cambridge, Mass.: M. I. T. Press, 1964.
     A description of the techniques for processing public opinion poll data studied by scientists for the Democratic Party.

299 Richter, Edward J., and Dulce, Berton. Religion and the Presidency: A Recurring American Problem.
     New York: Macmillan, 1962.
     Traces the evolution of the religious issue in American politics and concludes with five chapters on Kennedy's nomination, campaign, and election.

300 Schlesinger, Arthur M., Jr. Kennedy or Nixon: Does It Make a Difference? New York: Macmillan, 1960.
     A partisan pre-election analysis of the differences

between the two candidates. A book aimed at party
liberals.

301 Sevareid, Eric, ed. Candidates 1960: Behind the Head-
     lines in the Presidential Race. New York: Basic
     Books, 1959.
        A collection of essays on the major contenders for
     the presidential nominations in 1960 by national news-
     men.

     Sorensen, Theodore C. Kennedy. (See item 116.)

302 Tillet, Paul, ed. Inside Politics: The National Con-
     ventions, 1960. Dobbs Ferry, N. Y. : Oceana, 1962.
        A collection of studies by the Eagleton Institute
     of Politics on the state delegations, campaign organiza-
     tions, and nominations. Includes an analysis of Ken-
     nedy's role and tactics at the national convention.

     United States. Congress. Senate. Freedom of Com-
     munications.... (See items 48/9, 50, 51.)

303 Warren, Sidney. The Battle for the Presidency. Phil-
     adelphia: Lippincott, 1968.
        An analysis and description of ten presidential
     campaigns, including the 1960 one.

304 Weeks, Oliver D. Texas in the 1960 Presidential Elec-
     tion. Austin: Institute of Public Affairs, University
     of Texas Press, 1961. (Public Affairs Series, no.
     48.)

305 White, Theodore H. The Making of the President, 1960.
     New York: Atheneum, 1961.
        A best-selling, full account of the 1960 nomina-
     tions, campaigns, and election by a noted American
     historian who traveled with the candidates.

Part IV

KENNEDY ADMINISTRATION

GENERAL WORKS

306 Alexander, Herbert E. Money in Politics. Washington,
D. C. : Public Affairs Press, 1972.
A study of campaign financing based on the work
of the Commission on Campaign Costs established in
1961 by President Kennedy.

307 Allees, Arnold Edward. Tulips, Tears, Traumas &
Turmoil in the Kennedy Era. New York: Theo Gaus'
Sons, 1969.
The Kennedy era is depicted as glitter with little
substance, thus creating disillusionment.

308 Amrine, Michael. This Awesome Challenge. New
York: Putnam, 1964.
An account of L. B. Johnson's first 100 days as
President, including descriptions of the assassination,
the flight back to Washington, and the Kennedy staff
who served in Johnson's administration.

309 Anderson, Patrick. The Presidents' Men: White House
Assistants of Franklin D. Roosevelt, Harry S Truman,
Dwight D. Eisenhower, John F. Kennedy, and Lyndon
B. Johnson. Garden City, N. Y. : Doubleday, 1968.
Examines the roles of Lincoln, Schlesinger, Good-
win, Salinger, O'Donnell, O'Brien, Bundy, and Soren-
sen in the Kennedy administration.

310 Barber, James David. The Presidential Character:
Predicting Performance in the White House. Englewood Cliffs, N. J. : Prentice-Hall, 1972.
An analysis of four basic character models of
presidents; Kennedy is depicted as an "active-positive"
president.

311   Burns, James MacGregor.   Presidential Government:
      The Crucible of Leadership.   Boston: Houghton Miff-
      lin, 1966.
            Discusses three models of the presidency.   In-
      cludes an analysis of Kennedy's role in the office.

      Chase, Harold W. , and Lerman, Allen H.   Kennedy
      and the Press.   (See item 18.)

312   Christopherson, Edmund.   "Westward I Go Free"; The
      Story of J. F. K. in Montana.   Missoula, Mont. :
      Earthquake Press, 1964.

313   Comstock, Jim.   Pa and Ma and Mister Kennedy.   Rich-
      wood, W. Va. :   Appalachian Press, 1965.
            A narrative written in the dialect of a West Vir-
      ginia mountaineer about the President and his policies.

314   Cornwell, Elmer E.   Presidential Leadership of Public
      Opinion.   Bloomington: Indiana University Press,
      1965.
            An analysis of President Kennedy's use of the
      news media to mold public opinion.

315   Crown, James Tracy, and Penty, George P.   Kennedy
      in Power.   New York: Ballantine, 1961.
            A critical analysis of Kennedy's first few months
      in office.

316   David, Jay, ed.   The Kennedy Reader.   New York:
      Bobbs-Merrill, 1967.
            A collection of 50 well-known writings from books
      and articles by and about John F. Kennedy.

317   Day, J. Edward.   My Appointed Round: 929 Days as
      Postmaster General.   New York: Holt, Rinehart &
      Winston, 1965.
            Autobiography by Kennedy's Postmaster General.

318   Donald, Aida DiPace, ed.   John F. Kennedy and the
      New Frontier.   New York: Hill and Wang, 1966.
            A collection of writings by 19 noted authorities
      on Kennedy's presidency in terms of leadership, goals,
      and accomplishments.

319   Evans, M. Stanton; Ryskind, Allan H. ; and Schultz,
      William.   The Fringe on Top; Political Wildlife along

the New Frontier. New York: American Features, 1963.
A critique of the liberal influences and policies of the Kennedy administration in domestic and foreign affairs.

320 The Evening Star. The New Frontiersmen: Profiles of the Men around Kennedy. Washington, D. C.: Public Affairs Press, 1961.
Brief biographical sketches of over 300 New Frontiersmen.

321 Fagan, Myron C. The Kennedy Boys and Our Invisible Government. Hollywood, Calif.: Cinema Educational Guild, 1962.

322 Fagan, Myron C. Why Kennedy Must Be Impeached! Hollywood, Calif.: Cinema Educational Guild, 1962.

323 Fairlie, Henry. The Kennedy Promise: The Politics of Expectation. Garden City, N. Y.: Doubleday, 1972, 73.
A generally negative appraisal of President Kennedy's administration whose rhetoric fostered promises and expectations beyond his ability to deliver.

324 Fuchs, Lawrence H. John F. Kennedy and American Catholicism. New York: Meredith Press, 1967.
Historical perspectives and analysis of American attitudes towards Catholicism and the effect of the Kennedy campaign, election, and presidency.

325 Fuller, Helen. Year of Trial: Kennedy's Crucial Decisions. New York: Harcourt, Brace & World, 1962.
An analysis of Kennedy's first year in office and the critical decisions he faced.

326 Grossman, Richard L., ed. Let Us Begin: The First 100 Days of the Kennedy Administration. New York: Simon and Schuster, 1961.
A pictorial and written record of Kennedy's first 100 days in office.

327 Hanson, Galen A. A Summons for All Seasons; An Interpretive Study of President John F. Kennedy's Commencement Address at American University, June 10, 1963. Detroit: Harlo Press, 1966.
Introduction and commentary by the author.

328   Hartke, Vance, and Redding, John M.   Inside the New
      Frontier.   New York: McFadden-Bartell, 1962.
      A favorable interpretation of the Kennedy adminis-
      tration in terms of policies and programs.

329   Heath, Jim F.   Decade of Disillusionment: The Ken-
      nedy-Johnson Years.   Bloomington: Indiana University
      Press, 1975.
      A chronological account of the sixties emphasizing
      the optimism and promises which Presidents Kennedy
      and Johnson failed to fulfill.

330   Heller, Deane, and Heller, David.   The Kennedy Cabi-
      net; America's Men of Destiny.   Derby, Conn. :   Mon-
      arch, 1961.
      Brief biographical sketches of Kennedy's cabinet
      members.

331   Imlay, Robert.   The Cool War.   London: Mitre Press,
      1972.
      Essays on John, Robert, and Edward Kennedy.

332   Ions, Edmund S. , ed.   The Politics of John F. Kennedy.
      New York: Barnes & Noble, 1967.
      Writings by and about President Kennedy on his
      administration.   Appraisals by Richard Neustadt, Car-
      roll Kilpatrick, and William G. Carleton.

333   Johnson, Miles B.   The Government Secrecy Controversy.
      New York: Vantage, 1967.
      An examination of the presidential use of news
      media in the Eisenhower, Kennedy, and Johnson ad-
      ministrations.

334   Johnson, Richard T.   Managing the White House: An
      Intimate Study of Six Presidents.   New York: Harper
      & Row, 1974.
      A detailed study of the use of presidential as-
      sistants.

      Kennedy, John F.   President Kennedy's Program....
      (See item 33.)

335   Kluckhohn, Frank L.   America Listen!   An Honest Re-
      port to the Nation which Reveals That the Threat to
      Our Survival Is Greater Than Most Americans Have
      Been Permitted to Realize.   Derby, Conn. :   Monarch,
      1961.

336 Kluckhohn, Frank L. America Listen! An Up-to-the-
     Minute Report on the Chaos in Today's Washington.
     The Fumblings of the Kennedy Administration. The
     Search for Power. The Image Building. The Wield-
     ing of Influence on Business and the Press, rev. enl.
     ed. Derby, Conn. : Monarch, 1963.
     A rightist's critical appraisal of the President and
     his administration.

337 Kluckhohn, Frank L. America Listen! The Kennedy
     Administration and the Washington Scene--A Revealing
     Report on Power, Politics & Current Chaos in Our
     Federal Government. Derby, Conn. : Monarch, 1962.

338 Koenig, Louis W. The Chief Executive, rev. ed. New
     York: Harcourt, Brace & World, 1968.
     A comprehensive study of the presidency which
     includes an examination of Kennedy's administrative
     methods and role as party leader.

339 Kraft, Joseph. Profiles in Power: A Washington In-
     sight. New York: New American Library, 1966.
     An analysis of the people and institutions which
     form the power for political progress.

340 Lane, Thomas A. The Leadership of President Ken-
     nedy. Caldwell, Idaho: Caxton Printers, 1964.
     A negative appraisal of President Kennedy's lead-
     ership based on an interpretation of the President as
     too inexperienced and unprepared.

     Lasky, Victor. J. F. K. : The Man and the Myth.
     (See item 86.)

341 Latham, Earl. J. F. Kennedy and Presidential Power.
     Lexington, Mass. : Heath, 1972.
     A study of President Kennedy's exertion of lead-
     ership in both domestic and foreign affairs.

342 Lehdé, Norman B. , ed. When President Kennedy Vis-
     ited Pike County [Pa.]. Milford, Pa. : Pike County
     Chamber of Commerce, printed by Sun Litho-Press
     in East Stroudsburg, 1964.

     Lincoln, Evelyn. Kennedy & Johnson. (See item 90.)

     Lincoln, Evelyn. My Twelve Years with John F. Ken-
     nedy. (See item 91.)

343 Lord, Donald C.   John F. Kennedy; The Politics of
     Confrontation and Conciliation.   Woodbury, N.Y.:
     Barrow, 1975.
         An account of the life and times of JFK stressing
     his political career.   Includes chapters on image mak-
     ing and the verdict of history.

344 McGuiness, Kenneth C.   The New Frontier NLRB.
     Washington, D.C.:   Labor Policy Association, 1963.

345 Mailer, Norman.   The Presidential Papers.   New York:
     Putnam, 1963.
         A collection of papers addressed to the President
     on topics of national concern written by the noted au-
     thor.

     Manchester, William.   Portrait of a President....
     (See item 92.)

346 Mann, Dean E.   The Assistant Secretaries; Problems
     and Processes of Appointment.   Washington, D.C.:
     Brookings Institution, 1965.
         A study of appointments in the Eisenhower, Ken-
     nedy, and Johnson administrations.

347 Markmann, Charles Lam, and Sherwin, Mark.   John
     F. Kennedy: A Sense of Purpose.   New York: St.
     Martin's Press, 1961.
         An analysis and appraisal of Kennedy's first few
     months in office and a look at his goals for the future
     by two journalists.

348 Meyer, Karl E.   The New America; Politics and Soci-
     ety in the Age of the Smooth Deal.   New York: Basic
     Books, 1961.
         An analysis of politics and government at the be-
     ginning of the Kennedy administration.

349 Murray, Norbert.   Legacy of an Assassination.   New
     York: The Pro-People Press, 1964.
         An ultra-right, anti-Communist diatribe.   Views
     Kennedy's assassination as an awakening for the Amer-
     ican public to the "Red" dangers.

350 National Broadcasting System.   Memo to JFK from
     N.B.C. News.   New York: Putnam, 1961.
         An analysis of major problems facing the Kennedy
     administration by 11 N.B.C. correspondents.

O'Brien, Lawrence F. No Final Victories. (See item
18.)

O'Donnell; Powers; and McCarthy. "Johnny, We Hardly
Knew Ye. " (See item 99.)

351 Opotowsky, Stan. The Kennedy Government. London:
George G. Harrap & Co. , 1961.
Brief personal and political profiles of President
Kennedy, Vice President Johnson, and Cabinet mem-
bers interwoven with sketches on about fifty second-
line assistants.

Paper, Lewis. The Promise and the Performance.
(See item 100.)

352 Pollard, James E. The President and the Press, Truman to Johnson. Washington, D. C. : Public Affairs
Press, 1964.
A study of the relationships between the Presidents and the news media.

353 Polsby, Nelson, ed. The Modern Presidency. New
York: Random House, 1973.
A collection of writings on the presidency which
includes four articles on John Kennedy.

354 Republican National Committee. Research Division.
The Kennedy Log: A Daily Chronology of the Presidency of John F. Kennedy, January 20-December 31,
1961. Washington, D. C. : Republican National Committee, 1962.
A 161-page, indexed document.

Salinger, Pierre. With Kennedy. (See item 104.)

Schlesinger, Arthur M. , Jr. A Thousand Days. (See
item 107.)

355 Schnapper, Morris B. , ed. New Frontiers of the Kennedy Administration. Washington, D. C. : Public Affairs Press, 1961.
The reports of 12 task force studies on domestic
and foreign prepared for the Kennedy administration.

Schwab, Peter, and Sheidman, J. Lee. John F. Kennedy. (See item 108.)

Sidey, Hugh. John F. Kennedy, President. (See item
113.)

356   Smith, Malcolm E. Kennedy's 13 Great Mistakes in
the White House. New York: National Forum of
America, 1968.
Poses the thesis that JFK was ill-prepared for
the responsibility of the presidency, supported by an
interpretation of 13 major errors in decision-making.

357   Sorensen, Theodore C. Decision-Making in the White
House: The Olive Branch or the Arrows. New York:
Columbia University Press, 1961.
A descriptive book on the factors affecting presi-
dential decision-making written by Kennedy's special
counsel.

Sorensen, Theodore C. Kennedy. The Kennedy Legacy.
(See items 116, 117.)

358   Stanley, David T. Changing Administrations; The 1961
and 1964 Transitions in Six Departments. Washington, D.C.: Brookings Institution, 1965.
A study of the transitions in the departments of
State, Defense, Interior, Agriculture, H.E.W. and
the F.A.A.

359   Stuart, Roger Winship. The Thought Brigade: America's Influential Ghosts-in-Government. New York:
Obolensky, 1963.
Discusses the influence of academic and prossive
thinkers in the Kennedy administration.

360   Tanzer, Lester, ed. The Kennedy Circle. Washington, D.C.: Luce, 1961.
Political profiles of 19 men comprising Kennedy's
Cabinet, White House staff, and major advisors. Written by 14 national political reporters.

Thompson, Robert E., and Myers, Hortense. The
Brother Within. (See item 227.)

361   Tourtellot, Arthur B. The Presidents on the Presidency. Garden City, N.Y.: Doubleday, 1964.
Contains quotations from President Kennedy on
his concepts and attitudes towards the presidency.

362 United States. Congress. Senate. Summary of the
    Three-Year Kennedy Record and Digest of Major Ac-
    complishments of the 87th Congress and the 88th Con-
    gress, 1st Session, January 3, 1961 to December 30,
    1963. Washington, D.C.: U.S. Government Printing
    Office, 1964.

    United States. President. Public Papers of the Presi-
    dent.... (See items 52, 53, 54.)

363 Wise, David, and Ross, Thomas B. The Invisible
    Government. New York: Random House, 1964.
        An account of the American intelligence and es-
    pionage apparatus.

364 Wood Printing Works, Ltd. A Memory of John Fitz-
    gerald Kennedy: Visit to Ireland 26th-29th June, 1963.
    Dublin, Rep. of Ireland: Wood Printing Works, Ltd.,
    1963.
        An illustrated account of Kennedy's Presidential
    visit to Ireland. Foreword by Sean F. Lemass.

DOMESTIC AFFAIRS

365 Bolling, Richard. Power in the House; A History of
    the Leadership of the House of Representatives. New
    York: Dutton, 1968.
        The Missouri Congressman includes an account of
    JFK's relationship with the leadership of the House.

366 Canterbury, E. Ray. Economics on a New Frontier.
    Belmont, Calif.: Wadsworth, 1968.
        Presents the development of President Kennedy's
    understanding of economics and an appraisal of the
    economic policies of his administration.

367 Cater, Douglass. Power in Washington: A Critical
    Look at Today's Struggle to Govern in the Nation's
    Capital. New York: Random House, 1964.
        The national affairs editor of The Reporter
    examines the presidency, Congress, political parties,
    pressure groups, and the news media in their strug-
    gle for the power to govern.

368   Chapman, Gil, and Chapman, Ann. Who's Listening
      Now?   San Diego, Calif. :   Publishers Export Co. ,
      1967.
            An account of wiretapping and bugging emphasiz-
      ing the roles of Attorney General Robert F. Kennedy
      and F. B. I. Director J. Edgar Hoover.

369   Chase, Harold W.   Federal Judges: The Appointing
      Process.   St. Paul: University of Minnesota Press,
      1972.
            Includes a section on Kennedy appointees.   Based
      in part on interviews with Kennedy staff and appointees.

370   Elliff, John F.   Crime, Dissent, and the Attorney Gen-
      eral: The Justice Department in the 1960's.   Bever-
      ly Hills, Calif. :   Sage Publications, 1971.
            Examines the relationship between the attorney
      general and law enforcement.

371   Golden, Harry.   Mr. Kennedy and the Negroes.   Cleve-
      land: World Pub. Co. , 1964.
            A narrative on President Kennedy's role in the
      civil rights movement.

372   Goulden, Joseph C.   Meany.   New York: Atheneum,
      1972.
            Biography of the AFL-CIO President.   Includes
      a discussion of Kennedy and labor relations.

373   Hadwiger, Don Frank.   Pressures and Protests; The
      Kennedy Farm Program and the Wheat Referendum of
      1963.   San Francisco, Calif. :   Chandler Pub. Co. ,
      1965.
            A study developed from over 200 interviews.

374   Harris, Seymour.   Economics of the Kennedy Years
      and a Look Ahead.   New York: Harper & Row, 1964.
            A Harvard economist who served as an advisor to
      President Kennedy presents his interpretation of the
      people, problems, and programs determining economic
      policy during the Kennedy administration.

375   Harris, Seymour.   The Economics of the Political
      Parties, with Special Attention to Presidents Eisen-
      hower and Kennedy.   New York: Macmillan, 1962.
            A 1961 study on economic problems and efforts of
      the Kennedy administration to deal with them.

376 Heath, Jim F.   John F. Kennedy and the Business Com-
     munity. Chicago: University of Chicago Press, 1969.
     An economic history of the New Frontier.

377 Heller, Walter W.   New Dimensions of Political Econ-
     omy. Cambridge, Mass.: Harvard University Press,
     1966.
     An evaluation of President Kennedy's economic at-
     titudes and policies written by Kennedy's chairman of
     the Council of Economic Advisors.

378 Holtzman, Abraham.   Legislative Liaison: Executive
     Leadership in Congress. Chicago: Rand McNally,
     1970.
     Emphasizes the Kennedy administration's efforts
     to lead Congress.

379 Hoopes, Roy.   The Steel Crisis. New York: Day,
     1963.
     An analysis of President Kennedy's confrontation
     with the executives of the steel industry.

380 Hopkins, Thomas A. , ed.   Rights for Americans: The
     Speeches of Robert F. Kennedy. Indianapolis: Bobbs-
     Merrill, 1964.
     A collection of speeches on civil rights by RFK
     from 1961 to 1964.

381 Knapp, Daniel.   Scouting the War on Poverty: Social
     Reform Politics in the Kennedy Administration. Lex-
     ington, Mass.: Heath, 1971.
     A study of the factors determining social policy
     and legislation.

     Koch, Thilo.   Fighters for a New World. (See item
     85.)

382 Logsdon, John M.   The Decision to Go to the Moon:
     Project Apollo and the National Interest. Cambridge,
     Mass.: M. I. T. Press, 1970.
     An examination of the relationship between science
     and the national purpose, including a study of Ken-
     nedy's space policy.

383 Lord, Walter.   The Past that Would Not Die. New
     York: Harper & Row, 1965.
     An account of the Mississippi racial crisis over
     the admission of James Meredith to the University.

384 McConnell, Grant. Steel and the Presidency. New
     York: Norton, 1963.
        Examines the relationship between President Ken-
     nedy and the steel industry with particular reference
     to the controversy over increased prices.

385 Marris, Peter, and Rein, Martin. Dilemmas of Social
     Reform; Poverty and Community Action in the United
     States, 2d ed. Chicago: Aldine, 1973.
        An examination of the programs and projects de-
     veloped by the Juvenile Delinquency and Youth Of-
     fenses Control Act of 1961.

386 Marshall, Burke. Federalism and Civil Rights. New
     York: Columbia University Press, 1964.
        An analysis of the federal government and civil
     rights written by the assistant attorney general for
     the Civil Rights Division of the Department of Justice
     during the Kennedy administration.

387 Navasky, Victor S. Kennedy Justice. New York:
     Atheneum, 1971.
        A comprehensive study of Robert F. Kennedy as
     attorney general and the Department of Justice under
     his direction.

388 Norton, Hugh S. The Council of Economic Advisers;
     Three Periods of Influence. Columbia: Bureau of
     Business and Economic Research, University of South
     Carolina Press, 1973.
        A study of the Heller Council during the Kennedy
     years.

389 Nossiter, Bernard D. The Mythmakers: An Essay on
     Power & Wealth. Boston: Houghton Mifflin, 1964.
        An analysis of the economy in terms of the rela-
     tionship between labor, business, and the federal
     government during the Kennedy administration. Writ-
     ten by an economics reporter for the Washington Post.

     O'Hara, William T., ed. John F. Kennedy on Educa-
     tion. (See item 40.)

390 Rowen, Hobart. The Free Enterprisers: Kennedy,
     Johnson, and the Business Establishment. New York:
     Putnam, 1964.
        A detailed analysis of the relationship between the

Presidents and the business community written by a
leading economic reporter.

391 Rukeyser, Merryle Stanley. The Kennedy Recession:
A Complete Study of the Causes of Our Stagnating
Economy and Our Loss of World-Wide Prestige.
Derby, Conn. : Monarch, 1963.
A negative appraisal of Kennedy's economic ad-
visors, policies, and practices.

Saunders, Doris E., ed. The Kennedy Years and the
Negro. (See item 137.)

392 Silver, James W. Mississippi: The Closed Society.
New York: Harcourt, Brace & World, 1966.
An account of the federal-state crisis over the
admission of James Meredith, a Black student. Written by an eminent Southern historian and professor at
the University of Mississippi.

393 Sobel, Lester A., ed. Civil Rights, 1960-1966. New
York: Facts on File, 1967.
A collection of writings which chronicle the ma-
jor events in the civil rights movement.

394 Sundquist, James L. Politics and Policy: The Eisenhower, Kennedy, and Johnson Years. Washington,
D. C. : Brookings Institution, 1968.
Studies on six domestic problems and the solu-
tions by three different administrations.

395 Wamble, Thelma. Look Over My Shoulder; Letters
about President John F. Kennedy to John Allen Gould,
Grandson of John Fitzherbert Miller. New York:
Vantage, 1969.

396 Warren, Sidney. The President As World Leader.
Philadelphia: Lippincott, 1964.
An analysis of nine presidents, including JFK.

397 Westin, Alan F., ed. The Centers of Power: Three
Cases in American National Government. New York:
Harcourt, Brace & World, 1964.
Includes case studies on Kennedy's steel crisis
and aid-to-education bills.

398 Westin, Alan F., ed. The Uses of Power: Seven

Cases in American Politics.   New York: Harcourt,
Brace & World, 1962.
    One of the seven case studies, "Race, Religion,
and the Rules Committee: The Kennedy Aid-to-Education Bills," was written by Columbia University
Professor Hugh Douglas Price.

399 Wicker, Tom. JFK and LBJ: The Influence of Per-
     sonality upon Politics. New York: Morrow, 1968.
         A contrast of the personal attitudes and practices
     of Presidents Kennedy and Johnson by a New York
     Times political analyst.

400 Wiesner, Jerome. Where Science and Politics Meet.
     New York: McGraw-Hill, 1965.
         A collection of essays by Kennedy's special as-
     sistant for science and technology on the relationship
     between science and government.

401 Wilkens, B. H., and Friday, G. B., eds. The Eco-
     nomics of the New Frontier. New York: Random
     House, 1963.
         A collection of writings by Kennedy's major eco-
     nomic advisors.

FOREIGN AFFAIRS AND DEFENSE

GENERAL

402 Art, Robert J. The TFX Decision; McNamara and the
     Military. Boston: Little, Brown, 1968.
         A chronicle from 1959 through 1962 on the con-
     troversy of the TFX.

403 Attwood, William. The Reds and the Blacks. New
     York: Harper & Row, 1967.
         President Kennedy's ambassador to Guinea dis-
     cusses the Soviet and Chinese efforts in Africa and
     the American-African counter measures.

     Barbarash, Ernest E. John F. Kennedy on Israel.
     (See item 17.)

404 Bell, Coral. Negotiation from Strength: A Study in

the Politics of Power.   New York: Knopf, 1963.
Discusses U.S.-Soviet relations and Kennedy's
new initiatives in foreign policy.

405   Bloomfield, Lincoln P., et al.   Khrushchev and the
Arms Race.   Cambridge, Mass.:   M.I.T. Press,
1966.
Includes an analysis of the Soviet appraisal of
President Kennedy, his staff, and administration.

406   Bohlen, Charles E.   Witness to History, 1929-1969.
New York: Norton, 1973.
Autobiographical account of the author's life career with the Department of State.   Bohlen served as
foreign policy advisor and ambassador to France during the Kennedy administration.

407   Bowles, Chester.   Promises to Keep: My Years in
Public Life, 1941-1969.   New York: Harper & Row,
1971.
Autobiography of Ambassador Bowles, describing
his career with the Department of State.

408   Brennan, Donald G., ed.   Arms Control, Disarmament,
and National Security.   New York: Braziller, 1961.
A comprehensive exposition on arms control by
23 authoritative authors.   Revised and expanded version of the fall 1960 issue of Daedalus, the journal
of the American Academy of Arts and Sciences.

409   Brown, Seyom.   The Faces of Power; Constancy and
Change in United States Foreign Policy from Truman
to Johnson.   New York: Columbia University Press,
1968.
An analytical study of foreign policy premises by
a member of the Rand Corporation.

410   Clark, Keith C., and Legere, Laurence J., eds.   The
President and the Management of National Security:
A Report by the Institute for Defense Analyses.   New
York: Praeger, 1969.
Includes a discussion of Kennedy's use of national
security staff.

411   Cleveland, Harlan.   Great Power and Great Diversity:
The Perceptions and Policies of President Kennedy.
Washington, D.C.:   Department of State, 1964.
Views by a former assistant secretary of state.

412   Clubb, Oliver E., Jr.   The United States and the Sino-
      Soviet Bloc in Southeast Asia.   Washington, D. C.:
      Brookings Institution, 1963.
         An account of power-bloc competition in South-
      east Asia.

413   Cooper, Chester.   The Lost Crusade: America in
      Vietnam.   New York: Dodd Mead, 1970.
         An account written by an aide to McGeorge Bundy.

414   Cousins, Norman.   The Improbable Triumvirate: John
      F. Kennedy--Pope John--Nikita Khrushchev.   New
      York: Norton, 1972.
         Noted American author explains his role as an
      intermediary in seeking a rapprochement between Pope
      John and Premier Khrushchev as a basis for the Test
      Ban Treaty.

415   Curtis, Thomas B., and Vastine, John R.   The Ken-
      nedy Round and the Future of American Trade.   New
      York: Praeger, 1972.
         Presents and discusses the decisions that shaped
      American trade policy after the Trade Expansion Act
      of 1962.   Describes the methods of implementation.

416   Dean, Arthur H.   Test Ban and Disarmament: The
      Path of Negotiation.   New York: Harper & Row, 1966.
         The author served as Kennedy's chief negotiator
      at the Geneva Conference.   This study was published
      for the Council on Foreign Relations.

417   Destler, I. M.   Presidents, Bureaucrats and Foreign
      Policy.   Princeton, N. J.:   Princeton University
      Press, 1972.
         Includes an examination of President Kennedy's
      efforts to reform the Department of State.

418   Eliot, George Fielding.   Reserve Forces and the Ken-
      nedy Strategy.   Harrisburg, Pa.:   Stackpole, 1962.
         A brief and critical analysis of the role of the
      National Guard and Army Reserve in the Kennedy-
      McNamara military strategy of freedom of action.

419   Enthoven, Alain C., and Smith, K. Wayne.   How Much
      Is Enough?   Shaping the Defense Program 1961-1969.
      New York: Harper & Row, 1971.
         A study of the Department of Defense by authors

who served in the Department during the Kennedy administration.

420 Evans, John W. Kennedy Round in American Trade
Policy: The Twilight of the GAAT? Cambridge,
Mass.: Harvard University Press, 1971.
Review of American international trade policy with
specific treatment of the General Agreement on Tariffs
and Trade. The author led several delegations to
GAAT meetings.

421 FitzSimons, Louise. The Kennedy Doctrine. New
York: Random House, 1972.
A generally negative appraisal of Kennedy's foreign policy with an emphasis on counter-revolution
and counterinsurgency.

422 Fulbright, J. William. Old Myths and New Realities.
New York: Random House, 1964.
Commentaries on foreign relations based largely
on speeches by the chairman of the Senate Foreign
Relations Committee. Deals primarily with national
security, the Atlantic partnership, and the cold war.

423 Fulbright, J. William. Prospects for the West. New
York: Random House, 1963.
Views of the Democratic Senator who served as
chairman of the Foreign Relations Committee. Emphasis on U.S.-Soviet relations.

424 Galbraith, John Kenneth. Ambassador's Journal. Boston: Houghton Mifflin, 1969.
A personal account by Kennedy's ambassador to
India.

Galloway, John, ed. The Kennedys and Vietnam. (See
item 20.)

425 Godwin, Francis W.; Goodwin, Richard N.; and Haddad,
William F., eds. The Hidden Force. New York:
Harper & Row, 1963.
A collection of reports made at the International
Conference on Middle Level Manpower, sponsored by
the Peace Corps in San Juan, Puerto Rico, in 1962.
Includes statements by Wirtz, Heller, Shriver, and
Rostow, all of Kennedy's administration.

426   Goldwin, Robert A. , ed.   Why Foreign Aid?   Chicago:
      Rand McNally, 1962.
      Two messages by President Kennedy and essays
      by others concerning the nature and needs of foreign
      aid.

427   Goodfriend, Arthur.   The Twisted Image.   New York:
      St. Martin's Press, 1963.
      An appraisal of the United States Information
      Agency with an emphasis on India.

428   Goodwin, Richard N.   Triumph or Tragedy: Reflections
      on Vietnam.   New York: Random House, 1966.
      An account by a Kennedy advisor of the personal
      and human misjudgments that led to increased involve-
      ment in Vietnam.

429   Gromyko, Anatolii A.   Through Russian Eyes: Presi-
      dent Kennedy's 1036 Days.   Washington, D. C. :   In-
      ternational Library, 1973.
      A view of President Kennedy's policies, programs,
      and decision-making as a demonstration of a capital-
      istic philosophy.   Authored by the son of Soviet For-
      eign Minister Andrei Gromyko.

430   Halberstam, David.   The Best and the Brightest.   New
      York: Random House, 1969.
      An analysis of the men who advised Presidents
      Kennedy and Johnson on Vietnam policy.

431   Halberstam, David.   The Making of a Quagmire.   New
      York: Random House, 1964.
      An analysis of the American and South Vietnamese
      personalities and policies of the political, military,
      diplomatic, and news media corps in creating the in-
      soluble situation in Vietnam.
      A personal account of the author's 15 months in
      Vietnam as a correspondent for the New York Times.

      Hennessy, Maurice N.   I'll Come Back in the Spring-
      time.   (See item 81.)

432   Hilsman, Roger.   To Move a Nation: The Politics of
      Foreign Policy in the Administration of John F. Ken-
      nedy.   Garden City, N. Y. :   Doubleday, 1967.
      An analysis of personalities and policies in foreign
      affairs by an assistant secretary of state in Kennedy's
      administration.

433 Kahlin, G. M., and Lewis, J. W. The United States
     in Vietnam. New York: Delta, 1967.

434 Kaufmann, William W. The McNamara Strategy. New
     York: Harper & Row, 1964.
         An analysis of McNamara's role as secretary of
     defense.

435 Kennan, George. Memoirs, 1950-1963. Boston: Lit-
     tle, Brown, 1972.
         Autobiographic account of a career in the Depart-
     ment of State. Served as ambassador to Yugoslavia
     during Kennedy's administration.

     Kennedy, John F. Israel.... (See item 31.)

436 Kleiman, Robert. Atlantic Crisis: American Diplomacy
     Confronts a Resurgent Europe. New York: Norton,
     1964.
         Prepared originally as a private background paper
     for the Council on Foreign Relations. Discusses the
     failure of Kennedy's "Grand Design."

437 Kluckhohn, Frank. What's Wrong with U. S. Foreign
     Policy? Derby, Conn.: Monarch, 1963.
         A highly negative view of Kennedy's foreign policy.

438 Kolodziej, Edward A. The Uncommon Defense and Con-
     gress, 1945-1963. Columbus: Ohio State University
     Press, 1966.
         A study on the use of congressional appropria-
     tions as instruments of determining defense and for-
     eign policy.

439 Kraft, Joseph. The Grand Design: From Common
     Market to Atlantic Partnership. New York: Harper
     & Row, 1962.
         Explores the domestic and international implica-
     tions of Kennedy's plan for North American-Western
     European relations.

440 Lazo, Mario. Dagger in the Heart: American Policy
     Failures in Cuba. New York: Funk & Wagnalls,
     1968.
         Dr. Lazo is an American of Latin American par-
     entage who headed a law firm in Havana for 35 years.
     His book is an analysis of Castro's rise to power,

the Bay of Pigs, and the Cuban Missile Crisis; all of
which the author regards as failures in American foreign policy.

441   Lepper, Mary Milling. Foreign Policy Formulation: A
Case Study of the Nuclear Test Ban Treaty of 1963.
Columbus, Ohio: Merrill, 1971.
A study of the uses of public opinion and interest
groups with the Presidency and Congress in formulat-
ing foreign policy.

442   Levine, I. D. Eyewitness to History: Memoirs &
Reflections of a Foreign Correspondent for Half a
Century. New York: Hawthorn, 1973.

443   Liberty Lobby. Robert Strange McNamara, The True
Story of Dr. Strangebob. Washington, D. C. : Liberty
Lobby, 1967.
A right-wing critical interpretation of the Secre-
tary of Defense.

444   Lodge, Henry Cabot. The Storm Has Many Eyes; A
Personal Narrative. New York: Norton, 1973.
Includes a brief account of his tenure as ambas-
sador to Vietnam during the Kennedy administration.

445   McBride, James Hubert. The Test Ban Treaty: Mili-
tary, Technological, and Political Implications. Chicago: Regnery, 1967.
A study on future effects of the Nuclear Test Ban
Treaty.

446   MacFarquhar, Roderick, ed. Sino-American Relations,
1949-1971. New York: Praeger, 1972.
A documentary report of the Royal Institute of
International Affairs.

447   McKay, Vernon. Africa in World Politics. New York:
Harper & Row, 1963.
Briefly discusses United States foreign policy to-
wards Africa during the Kennedy administration.

448   MacMillan, Harold. At the End of the Day, 1961-1963.
New York: Harper & Row, 1973.
Great Britain's Prime Minister discusses his re-
lationship with President Kennedy.

449   McNamara, Robert S.   The Essence of Security: Re-
      flections in Office.   New York: Harper & Row, 1968.
      Kennedy's Secretary of Defense writes about the
      tools of power and the meaning of security.

450   McSherry, James E.   Khrushchev and Kennedy in Retro-
      spect.   Arlington, Va.: Open-Door Press, 1972.
      An examination of the relationship and conflicts be-
      tween the two world leaders, emphasizing the Berlin
      and Cuban crises.

451   Marshall, Robert A., ed.   Kennedy and Africa.   New
      York: Pyramid Books, 1967.
      Statements by President Kennedy on Africa.

452   Martin, John Bartlow.   Overtaken by Events.   Garden
      City, N.Y.: Doubleday, 1966.
      An account by Kennedy's ambassador to the Do-
      minican Republic.

453   Mecklin, John.   Mission in Torment.   Garden City,
      N.Y.: Doubleday, 1965.
      An "inside" report on the causes of American
      errors in Vietnam policy estimates by a former sen-
      ior U.S. diplomat in Saigon.

454   Neustadt, Richard E.   Alliance Politics.   New York:
      Columbia University Press, 1970.
      Examines United States foreign policy toward
      Great Britain with reference to the Suez crisis and
      the cancellation of Skybolt.

455   Nunnerley, David.   President Kennedy and Britain.
      New York: St. Martin's Press, 1972.
      An analysis of Anglo-American relations in the
      Kennedy-Macmillan era by an associate of the Royal
      Institute of International Affairs.

456   Paranjoti, Violet.   President John F. Kennedy; Crea-
      tive Statesmanship in the Field of Foreign Affairs.
      New York: Carlton, 1965.

457   Preeg, Ernest H.   Traders and Diplomats; An Analysis
      of the Kennedy Round of Negotiations under the Gen-
      eral Agreement on Tariffs and Trade.   Washington,
      D.C.: Brookings Institution, 1970.
      A chronological study and evaluation of the nego-

tiations by the author, a member of the U. S. delega-
tion. In May 1960 over 600 delegates from 82 nations
negotiated on increasing trade and decreasing tariffs
for developing nations.

458   Raskin, Marcus G. , and Fall, Bernard B. , eds.   The
      Viet-Nam Reader: Articles and Documents on Amer-
      ican Foreign Policy and the Viet-Nam Crisis.   New
      York: Random House, 1965.
          Contains nearly 50 articles or documents by noted
      journalists, academicians, and government officials.
      Includes a chronology of events, a selective bibliogra-
      phy, and biographical data on contributors.

459   Roherty, James M.   Decisions of Robert S. McNamara.
      Coral Gables, Fla. :   University of Miami Press,
      1970.
          Examines the impact of McNamara's decisions on
      the office of secretary of defense.

460   Rostow, W. W.   The Diffusion of Power; An Essay in
      Recent History.   New York: Macmillan, 1972.
          Emphasis on the Kennedy and Johnson years.
      Written by a White House advisor on foreign policy
      to JFK and LBJ.

461   Rusk, Dean.   Winds of Freedom.   Boston: Beacon,
      1963.
          Speeches and statements made by the Secretary
      of State from January 1961 to August 1962.

462   Schwartz, Abba P.   The Open Society.   New York:
      Morrow, 1968.
          A narrative on immigration reform and freedom
      of travel by Kennedy's administrator of the Bureau of
      Security and Consular Affairs.

463   Simpson, Smith.   Anatomy of the State Department.
      Boston: Houghton Mifflin, 1967.
          A critical study of the Department of State by a
      career official of government service.

464   Singh, Ram, and Haldar, M. K. , eds.   Kennedy
      through Indian Eyes.   New York: International Pub.
      Services, 1964.
          A selection of speeches and statements about India
      and foreign policy with a biographical introduction by
      the authors.

465 Sobel, Lester A., ed. Disarmament and Nuclear Tests,
     1960-1963. New York: Facts on File, 1964.
     A collection of journalistic writings.

466 Sorensen, Thomas C. The Word War: The Story of
     American Propaganda. New York: Harper & Row,
     1968.
     A narrative on the United States Information
     Agency during the Kennedy administration by a mem-
     ber of the Agency. The author is the brother of
     Theodore C. Sorensen.

467 Taylor, Maxwell D. Swords and Plowshares. New
     York: Norton, 1972.
     Autobiography of General Taylor who served as
     military advisor to President Kennedy and chairman
     of the Joint Chiefs of Staff during the Kennedy ad-
     ministration.

468 Terchek, Ronald J. The Making of the Test Ban Treaty.
     The Hague: Nijhoff, 1970.
     A study on the interrelationship between the Pres-
     ident, Congress, the media, and the public in the pur-
     suit of the treaty.

469 Walton, Richard J. Cold War and Counter-Revolution:
     The Foreign Policy of John F. Kennedy. New York:
     Viking, 1972.
     An interpretation of Kennedy's role in foreign
     policy basically as a cold warrior and a counter-
     revolutionary.

470 Weissman, Stephen R. American Policy in the Congo,
     1960-1964. Ithaca, N. Y.: Cornell University, 1974.
     An account of the Kennedy administration's poli-
     cies and actions toward the developing countries in
     the Congo.

471 Williams, G. Mennen. Africa for the Africans. Grand
     Rapids, Mich.: Eerdmans, 1969.
     An examination of the independence movements
     written by Kennedy's assistant secretary of state for
     Africa.

     Wszelaki, Jan H., ed. John F. Kennedy and Poland.
     (See item 56.)

ALLIANCE FOR PROGRESS

472 Drier, John C., ed. The Alliance for Progress: Problems and Perspectives. Baltimore, Md.: Johns Hopkins University Press, 1962.
A series of lectures on United States-Latin American relations.

473 Gordon, Lincoln. A New Deal for Latin America: The
Alliance for Progress. Cambridge, Mass.: Harvard
University Press, 1963.
An explanation of the purposes, philosophy, and
methods of the Alliance for Progress by one of its
chief architects, Kennedy's ambassador to Brazil.

474 Levinson, Jerome, and de Onis, Juan. The Alliance
that Lost Its Way: A Critical Report on the Alliance
for Progress. Chicago: Quadrangle, 1970.

475 Nystrom, John Warren. The Alliance for Progress.
New York: Van Nostrand, 1966.

476 Perloff, Harvey S. Alliance for Progress: A Social
Invention in the Making. Baltimore: Johns Hopkins
University Press, 1969.

BERLIN

477 Dulles, Eleanor L. The Wall: A Tragedy in Three
Acts. Columbia: University of South Carolina Press,
1972. (Studies in International Affairs, no. 9.)

478 Heller, Deane, and Heller, David. The Berlin Crisis.
Derby, Conn.: Monarch, 1961.
Foreword by Konrad Adenauer. An interpretive
narrative examining the issues and Khrushchev's de-
mands.

479 Keller, John Wendell. Germany, The Wall and Berlin:
International Politics during an International Crisis.
New York: Vantage, 1964.
Introduction by Hans Kohn.

480 Mander, John. Berlin, Hostage for the West. Baltimore: Penguin, 1962.

481   Schick, Jack M.   The Berlin Crisis, 1958-1962.   Phila-
      delphia: University of Pennsylvania Press, 1971.
      A study of the Berlin crisis including the impact
      of the Cuban missile crisis.

482   Slusser, Robert M.   The Berlin Crisis of 1961; Soviet-
      American Relations and the Struggle for Power in the
      Kremlin, June-November 1961.   Baltimore: Johns
      Hopkins University Press, 1973.
      An examination of the Berlin crisis including an
      analysis of Soviet foreign policy.

483   Windsor, Philip.   City on Leave: A History of Berlin
      1945-1962.   New York: Praeger, 1963.
      A comprehensive study which includes an account
      of Kennedy's handling of the Berlin crisis.

                              CUBA

484   Abel, Elie.   The Missiles of October; The Story of the
      Cuban Missile Crisis 1962.   London: MacGibbon &
      Kee, 1969.
      An account of the Cuban missile crisis by a noted
      foreign correspondent for the New York Times and
      N. B. C. news.   This book was published in 1966 under
      the title, The Missile Crisis.

485   Allison, Graham T.   Essence of Decision: Explaining
      the Cuban Missile Crisis.   Boston: Little, Brown,
      1971.
      The author uses three conceptual models to ex-
      plain how the administration handled the crisis.

486   Bayard, James [pseud.].   The Real Story on Cuba.
      Derby, Conn. :   Monarch, 1963.
      A journalistic chronicle of the 1962 crisis.

487   Chayes, Abram.   The Cuban Missile Crisis: Interna-
      tional Crisis and the Role of Law.   New York: Ox-
      ford, 1974.
      An explanation of the role of international law in
      handling the missile crisis by a legal advisor to the
      Department of State during the crisis.

488   Daniel, James, and Hubbell, John G.   Strike in the
      West: The Complete Story of the Cuban Crisis.   New

York: Holt, Rinehart & Winston, 1963.
A reconstruction of the events of the Cuban missile crisis.

489   Divine, Robert A. , ed.   The Cuban Missile Crisis.
New York: Quadrangle, 1971.
A selection of writings by government officials,
political scientists, and journalists.

490   Fagan, Myron C.   Must We Have a Cuban "Pearl Har-
bor?" Hollywood, Calif.:   Cinema Educational Guild,
1962.
A rightist, anti-Kennedy presentation.

491   Foreign Policy Association.   The Cuban Crisis: A
Documentary Record.   New York: Foreign Policy
Association, 1963.   (Headline Series, no. 157.)
Selected documentation and chronology of events.

492   Freeman, Thomas [pseud.].   The Crisis in Cuba.
Derby, Conn.:   Monarch, 1963.
Presents a brief overview of the 1962 confronta-
tion.

493   Halper, Thomas.   Foreign Policy Crises: Appearance
and Reality in Decision Making.   Columbus, Ohio:
Merrill, 1971.
Uses five case studies including the Bay of Pigs
invasion and the Cuban missile crisis.

494   Hammarskjold Forum.   The Inter-American Security
System and the Cuban Crisis.   Dobbs Ferry, N.Y.:
Oceana, 1964.
Reports and proceedings of the Third Hammar-
skjold Forum, November 1962.

495   Hermann, Charles F.   Crises in Foreign Policy: A
Simulation Analysis.   New York: Bobbs-Merrill,
1969.
Simulation studies of the South Korean invasion
and the Cuban missile crisis are used to define crisis
and test hypotheses.

496   Holsti, Ole R.   Crisis, Escalation, War.   Montreal:
McGill-Queens University Press, 1972.
An analysis of policy-making under high stress,
exemplified by World War I and the Cuban missile
crisis.

497   Johnson, Haynes.   The Bay of Pigs: The Invasion of
      Cuba by Brigade 2506.   London: Hutchinson, 1964.
         An account of the Bay of Pigs invasion based on
      interviews with men in the Cuban brigade.

498   Kennedy, Robert F.   Thirteen Days: A Memoir of the
      Cuban Missile Crisis.   New York: Norton, 1969.
         The personal account of RFK on the handling of
      the Cuban missile crisis.   Emphasizes personalities,
      ideologies, and events that shaped decision-making.

499   Larson, David L. , ed.   The Cuban Crisis of 1962, Se-
      lected Documents and Chronology.   Boston: Houghton
      Mifflin, 1963.
         A compilation of important materials on the mis-
      sile crisis.

500   Matthews, Herbert Lionel.   The Cuban Story.   New
      York: Braziller, 1961.
         First-hand account by a New York Times cor-
      respondent.

501   Meyer, Karl E. , and Szulc, Tad.   The Cuban Invasion:
      The Chronicle of a Disaster.   New York: Praeger,
      1962.
         A detailed and documented account of the events
      of the Bay of Pigs invasion by New York Times jour-
      nalists.

502   Pachter, Henry M.   Collision Course: The Cuban Mis-
      sile Crisis and Coexistence.   New York: Praeger,
      1963.
         A study of international relations in the missile
      crisis.

503   Phillips, Ruby Hart.   The Cuban Dilemma.   New York:
      Obolensky, 1963.
         A chronicle of social, political, and economic de-
      velopments in Cuba from 1960 through May 1961 by
      a New York Times correspondent.

504   Russell, Bertrand R.   Unarmed Victory.   New York:
      Simon and Schuster, 1963.
         Presents a discussion of the Cuban missile crisis
      and the Sino-Indian border conflict.

505   Smith, Robert Freeman.   What Happened in Cuba? A
      Documentary History.   New York: Twayne, 1963.

506 Sobel, Lester A. , ed. Cuba, the U.S. & Russia
     1960-1963. New York: Facts on File, 1964.
       A collection of journalistic writings on events and
     relations between the three nations.

507 Tanner, Hans. Counter-Revolutionary Agent: Diary of
     the Events which Occurred in Cuba between January
     and July, 1961. London: G. T. Foulis, 1962.
       Narrative on the Bay of Pigs invasion.

508 Weintal, Edward, and Bartlett, Charles. Facing the
     Brink: An Intimate Study of Crisis Diplomacy. New
     York: Charles Scribner's Sons, 1967.
       An examination of personalities and methods in
     handling international crisis. One of the five crises
     studied is the Cuban missile crisis.

509 Wisan, Joseph E. The Cuban Crisis as Reflected in
     the New York Press. New York: Octagon Books,
     1965. (Columbia University, Columbia Studies in the
     Social Sciences.)

510 Zeitlin, Maurice, and Sheer, Robert. Cuba: Tragedy
     in Our Hemisphere. New York: Grove, 1963.

                           PEACE CORPS

511 Adams, Velma. The Peace Corps in Action. Chicago:
     Follett, 1968.
       An analysis of the limitations and successes of
     the first two years of the Peace Corps.

512 Albertson, Maurice L.; Riche, Andrew E.; and Birky,
     Pauline E. New Frontiers for American Youth:
     Perspectives on the Peace Corps. Washington, D.C. :
     Public Affairs Press, 1961.

513 American Academy of Political and Social Science.
     The Peace Corps. New York: The Academy, 1965.

514 Armstrong, Roger D. Peace Corps and Christian Mis-
     sion. New York: Friendship Press, 1965.
       Narrative by a volunteer.

515 Ashabranner, Brent. A Moment in History: The First
     Ten Years of the Peace Corps. Garden City, N. Y. :

Doubleday, 1974.
A Peace Corps worker in Nigeria and India traces
the history of the Corps.

516   Brooks, Rhoda S., and Brooks, E. G.   The Barrios
of Manta; A Personal Account of the Peace Corps in
Ecuador.   New York: New American Library, 1965.
Highlights social, economic, and cultural differ-
ences.

517   Carey, Robert G.   The Peace Corps.   New York:
Praeger, 1971.
Describes the background and operating structure
of the Peace Corps.   Text accompanied by photographs,
organizational charts and tables.

518   Cowan, Paul.   The Making of an Un-American; A Dia-
logue with Experience.   New York: Viking, 1970.
The author, a Peace Corps volunteer, discusses
the failures of the Peace Corps and his own development from liberalism to radicalism.

519   Dupree, Louis.   The Peace Corps in Afghanistan: The
Impact of Volunteers on the Country and the Country
on the Volunteers.   New York: American Universities
Field Staff, Inc., 1964.

520   Ezickson, Aaron Jacob.   The Peace Corps; A Pictorial
History.   New York: Hill & Wang, 1965.
Introduction by Sargent Shriver, first director of
the Peace Corps.

521   Fuchs, Lawrence H.   Those Peculiar Americans.   New
York: Meredith, 1967.
A volume on the motivations and work of volunteers by a former Peace Corps director in the Philip-
pines.

522   Hapgood, David, and Bennett, Meridan.   Agents of
Change: A Close Look at the Peace Corps.   Boston:
Little, Brown, 1968.
A book depicting the merits of the Peace Corps.

523   Harris, Mark.   Twenty-One Twice: A Journal.   Boston:
Little, Brown, 1966.
A personal account by a Peace Corps volunteer.

524   Hayes, Samuel P.   An International Peace Corps: The
      Promise and the Problems.   Washington, D.C.:   Pub-
      lic Affairs Press, 1961.

525   Hoopes, Roy.   The Complete Peace Corps Guide, rev.
      ed.   New York: Dial, 1965.
      A factual introduction to the Peace Corps by a
      Washington correspondent.   Foreword by R. Sargent
      Shriver.

526   Hoopes, Roy.   The Peace Corps Experience.   New
      York: Potter, 1967.
      Describes the value of the Peace Corps work for
      those in the host countries and for the volunteers.

527   James, Josephine.   Peace Corps Nurse.   New York:
      Golden Press, 1965.

528   Kittler, Glenn D.   The Peace Corps.   New York:
      Paperback Library, 1963.
      A brief account of the formation and operation of
      the Peace Corps in its first two years.

529   Knebel, Fletcher.   The Zin-Zin Road.   Garden City,
      N.Y.:   Doubleday, 1966.

530   Lavine, David, and Mandelbaum, Ira.   What Does a
      Peace Corps Volunteer Do?   New York: Dodd, Mead,
      1966.

531   Leavitt, Leonard.   An African Season.   New York:
      Simon and Schuster, 1967.
      A personal account by a volunteer in Tanzania.

532   Luce, Iris, ed.   Letters from the Peace Corps.   Wash-
      ington, D.C.:   Luce, 1964.
      A collection of 28 letters from Peace Corps volun-
      teers depicting life in the Corps from training to the
      field of operation.   A few editorial comments included.

533   Madow, Pauline, ed.   The Peace Corps.   New York:
      H. W. Wilson Co., 1964.   (The Reference Shelf, vol.
      36, no. 2.)
      A brief account of the formation and mission of
      the Peace Corps.

534   Obi, Enuenwemba.   Peace Corpism.   New York: Pag-
      eant, 1966.

535 Pagano, Jules. Education in the Peace Corps; Evolving
     Concepts of Volunteer Training. New York: Center
     for the Study of Liberal Education, 1965.

536 Powell, Richard. Don Quixote U. S. A. New York:
     Scribner's, 1966.

537 Rogers, David. The Peace Corps Girls: A Play in
     Three Acts. Chicago: Dramatic Pub. Co., 1962.

538 Sayers, William. Do Good. New York: Holt, Rine-
     hart & Winston, 1966.

539 Shriver, R. Sargent. Point of the Lance. New York:
     Harper & Row, 1964.
     A selection of speeches and articles by the Presi-
     dent's brother-in-law and first director of the Peace
     Corps. Includes speeches on the formation and early
     development of the Peace Corps.

540 Shurtleff, William. Peace Corps Year with Nigerians.
     Frankfurt, Germany: Moritz Desterweg, 1966.

541 Smith, Ed. Where To, Black Man? Chicago: Quad-
     rangle, 1967.

542 Spencer, Sharon. Breaking the Bonds. New York:
     Tempo Books, 1963.

543 Stein, Morris I. Volunteers for Peace; The First
     Group of Peace Corps Volunteers in a Rural Commun-
     ity Development Program in Colombia, South America.
     New York: Wiley, 1966.

544 Sullivan, George. The Story of the Peace Corps. New
     York: Fleet, 1964.
     A review of the history, membership, selection
     and training, and projects and programs of the Peace
     Corps.

545 Textor, Robert B., ed. Cultural Frontiers of the Peace
     Corps. Cambridge, Mass.: M. I. T. Press, 1966.
     A collection of writings on cultural impact. In-
     troduction by Margaret Mead, renowned Columbia
     University professor of anthropology.

546 Thomsen, Moritz. Living Poor: A Peace Corps Chron-

icle.   Seattle, Wash.:   University of Washington
Press, 1969.
Personal narrative by a Peace Corps volunteer.

547   Unger, Marvin H.   Paw Paw, Foo Foo, and Ju Ju:
Recollections of a Peace Corps Volunteer.   New York:
Citadel, 1968.

548   United States.   Peace Corps.   The Peace Corps Reader.   New York: Quadrangle, 1967.
A collection of 20 articles published for prospec-
tive volunteers.

549   United States.   Peace Corps.   The Peace Corps Reader.   Washington, D.C.:   U.S. Peace Corps, 1968.
An anthology of 28 essays, several by volunteers
of the Corps.

550   Weiss, Alan.   High Risk/High Gain.   New York: St.
Martin's Press, 1968.

551   Whittlesey, Susan.   Good Will toward Men: The Challenge of the Peace Corps.   New York: Coward-Mc-
Cann, 1963.

552   Whittlesey, Susan.   U.S. Peace Corps.   New York:
Coward-McCann, 1963.

553   Wiley, Karla.   Assignment Latin America: A Story of
the Peace Corps.   New York: McKay, 1968.

554   Windmiller, Marshall.   The Peace Corps and Pax Amer-
icana.   Washington, D.C.:   Public Affairs Press,
1970.
A view of the Peace Corps as an extension of im-
perialistic American policy.

555   Wingenbach, Charles E.   Peace Corps.   New York:
McGraw-Hill, 1965.

556   Wingenbach, Charles E.   The Peace Corps; Who, How
and Where.   New York: Day, 1962.
Examines the history, selection and training of
volunteers, and organization and administration in host
countries.   Foreword by Hubert Humphrey.

557   Zeitlin, Arnold.   To the Peace Corps, with Love.
Garden City, N.Y.:   Doubleday, 1965.

DESCRIPTIONS

558 Baker, Dean C. The Assassination of President Kennedy: A Study of the Press Coverage. Ann Arbor: University of Michigan Department of Journalism, 1965.

559 Baughman, E. U., and Robinson, Leonard Wallace. Secret Service Chief. New York: Harper & Row, 1961, 1962.
Contains brief sections on the Kennedy assassination attempt in Palm Beach and the assassination in Dallas.

560 Bennett, Arnold. Jackie, Bobby & Manchester: The Story behind the Headlines. New York: Bee-Line Books, 1967.
An account of the dispute over the publication of The Death of a President by Manchester (see item 578).

561 Bishop, Jim. The Day Kennedy Was Shot. New York: Funk & Wagnalls, 1968.
An hour-by-hour account of the persons and events related to the assassination of President Kennedy.

562 Bloomgarden, Henry S. The Gun: A "Biography" of the Gun That Killed John F. Kennedy. New York: Grossman, 1975.
A history of the Mannlicher-Carcano purchased by Oswald.

563 Brooks, Stewart M. Our Murdered Presidents: The Medical Story. New York: Fell, 1966.

An account of the medical aspects related to the
deaths of the four assassinated American presidents.

564 Corry, John. The Manchester Affair. New York:
     Putnam, 1967.
         An account of the dispute over the publication of
     The Death of a President (see item 578). Written by
     a New York Times reporter.

565 Cottrell, John. Anatomy of Assassination. London:
     Muller, 1966.

566 Cottrell, John. Assassination! The World Stood Still.
     London: New English Library, 1964.

567 Denson, R. B. , comp. Destiny in Dallas: Assassin
     and Assassin's Assassin. Dallas: Denco Corp. ,
     1964.
         A 64-page book on Lee Harvey Oswald and Jack
     Ruby.

568 Donoghue, Mary Agnes. Assassination: Murder in
     Politics. Chatsworth, Calif. : Major Books, 1975.
         Contains a 40-page chapter on the President's
     death in Dallas.

569 Gay, Donovan L. , ed. The Assassination of President
     John F. Kennedy: The Warren Commission Report
     and Subsequent Interest. Washington, D. C. : Library
     of Congress, 1975.
         A 38-page government publication reviewing the
     assassination events and the Warren Commission as
     well as subsequent public and governmental interest
     in the investigation. Selected references included.

570 Greenberg, Bradley S. , and Parker, Edwin B. , eds.
     The Kennedy Assassination and the American Public:
     Social Communication in Crisis. Stanford, Calif. :
     Stanford University Press, 1965.
         A collection of studies on how people heard about
     the assassination, their immediate and subsequent
     reactions, and the effects on political beliefs.

571 Gun, Nerin E. Red Roses from Texas. London:
     Frederick Muller, 1964.
         A French journalist's detailed account of the
     events of November 22, 1963.

572   Habe, Hans.   The Wounded Land: Journey through a
      Divided America.   New York: Coward-McCann, 1964.
      A noted American-European journalist and novelist
      reports on salient American attitudes and character-
      istics immediately preceding and following the assas-
      sination.

573   Henderson, Bruce, and Summerlin, Sam.   1:33 In
      Memoriam: John F. Kennedy.   New York: Cowles
      Education Corp. , 1968.
      An account of people's reactions to the news of
      President Kennedy's death.

      Jenkins, John H.   Neither the Fanatics nor the Faint-
      hearted.   (See item 26.)

574   Knight, Janet, ed.   Three Assassinations: The Deaths
      of John and Robert Kennedy and Martin Luther King.
      New York: Facts on File, 1971.
      An illustrated review of the highlights of the three
      assassinations.

575   Leslie, Warren.   Dallas Public and Private.   New
      York: Grossman, 1964.
      A descriptive book on the city of Dallas at the
      time of Kennedy's assassination.   Authored by a
      Dallas reporter and businessman.

576   McConnell, Brian.   Assassination.   London: Leslie
      Frewin Pub. , 1969.
      An English reporter's history of world assassina-
      tions.   Includes one chapter on President Kennedy's
      death in Dallas.

577   McKinley, James.   Assassination in America.   New
      York: Harper & Row, 1977.
      A history of the major assassinations in the
      United States which includes an account of President
      Kennedy's death in Dallas and the primary features
      of a number of conspiratorial theories.   Also pre-
      sents an account of the Robert Kennedy assassination
      in Los Angeles.

578   Manchester, William.   The Death of a President.   New
      York: Harper & Row, 1967.
      An extensive account of the death of President
      Kennedy covering the days November 20 to November

25, 1963. Based on over 300 interviews, including
Kennedy family and close associates.

579 Matthews, James P. , et al. The Complete Kennedy
Saga. Los Angeles: Associated Professional Ser-
vices, 1963.
A collection of four collector's edition books:
Four Dark Days; Assassination: The Lee Harvey Os-
wald Biography; Highlights of the Warren Report:
The Facts Surrounding the Assassination of John F.
Kennedy; and In Memoriam.

580 Matthews, James P. , ed. Four Dark Days in History;
A Photo History of President Kennedy's Assassination.
Los Angeles: Associated Professional Services, 1963.

581 Mayo, John B. Bulletin from Dallas: The President
Is Dead; The Story of John F. Kennedy's Assassination
As Covered by Radio and TV. Hicksville, N. Y. :
Exposition, 1967.

582 Murphy, Lois Barclay, and Moriarty, Alice E. Vulner-
ability, Coping and Growth from Infancy to Adoles-
cence. New Haven, Conn. : Yale University Press,
1975.
Includes a study on children's reactions to the
assassination of President Kennedy. Part of the comprehensive longitudinal studies on children research
at the Menninger Foundation.

583 National Broadcasting Co. Seventy Hours and Thirty
Minutes. New York: Random House, 1966.
An abbreviated, but not edited, transcript of the
N. B. C. television broadcast on the Kennedy assassina-
tion and funeral.

584 National Broadcasting Co. There Was a President.
New York: Random House and Ridge Press, 1966.
An illustrated version of Seventy Hours and Thirty
Minutes (item 583), the minute-by-minute log of Ken-
nedy's assassination and funeral by N. B. C.

585 New York Times, Editors of. Assassination of a President. New York: Viking, 1964.
A compilation of most of the newspaper articles
published on the assassination and its aftermath by the
New York Times.

586   United Press International and American Heritage, Ed-
      itors of, comps.   Four Days: The Historical Record
      of the Death of President Kennedy.   New York: Amer-
      ican Heritage, 1964.
         A pictorial record with text covering the four days
      of Kennedy's assassination and funeral.

587   Van Gelder, Lawrence.   The Untold Story: Why the
      Kennedys Lost the Book Battle.   New York: Award
      Books, 1967.
         An account of the Kennedy-Manchester book feud
      (concerning item 578).

588   Wilson, Frank J., and Day, Beth.   Special Agent: A
      Quarter Century with the Treasury Department and the
      Secret Service.   New York: Holt, Rinehart & Win-
      ston, 1965.
         Autobiography by a former Secret Service chief
      which includes two brief references to President
      Kennedy and his assassination.

589   Wise, Dan, and Maxfield, Marietta.   The Day Kennedy
      Died.   San Antonio, Tex.:   Naylor, 1964.
         A recreation of the events in Dallas on November
      22, 1963, by two Dallas residents.

590   Wolfenstein, Martha, and Kliman, Gilbert, eds.   Chil-
      dren and the Death of a President.   Garden City,
      N.Y.:   Doubleday, 1965.
         A collection of nine case studies on children and
      the impact of President Kennedy's death.   Research
      conducted by behavioral and social scientists.

591   Youngblood, Rufus W.   Twenty Years in the Secret Ser-
      vice.   New York: Simon and Schuster, 1974.
         Memoirs of the Secret Service Agent guarding
      Vice President Johnson in the Dallas motorcade.

INVESTIGATION

592   Bonner, Judith Whitson.   Investigation of a Homicide:
      The Murder of John F. Kennedy.   Anderson, S.C.:
      Droke House, 1969.
         An account of the investigation by the Dallas Po-
      lice Force.

593   Commission on C. I. A. Activities.   The Nelson Rocke-
      feller Report to the President.   New York: Manor
      Books, 1975.
          One chapter of the report deals with the allega-
      tion concerning the assassination of President Kennedy.

594   Curry, Jesse.   JFK: Assassination File.   Dallas:
      American Poster and Printing Co., 1969.
          An account of the investigation written by the Dal-
      las Chief of Police.

595   Johnson, Marion M., comp.   Preliminary Inventory of
      the Records of the President's Commission on the
      Assassination of President Kennedy.   Washington,
      D. C.:   National Archives and Records Service, Gen-
      eral Services Administration, 1970.
          A 28-page listing.

596   Kirkham, James F.; Levy, Sheldon G.; and Crotty,
      William J.   Assassination and Political Violence: A
      Staff Report to the National Commission on the Causes
      and Prevention of Violence.   New York: Bantam,
      1970.
          A presentation of the multi-disciplinary studies
      and findings on American assassination and political
      violence.

597   Lifton, David S., comp.   Document Addendum to the
      Warren Report.   El Segundo, Calif.:   Sightext Publi-
      cations, 1968.
          Contains the declassified transcripts of the execu-
      tive sessions of the Warren Commission, the first
      tape recorded interrogation of Marina Oswald, and
      the Liebeler Memorandum on galley proofs for chap-
      ter IV of the Warren Report.

598   Meagher, Sylvia.   Subject Index to the Warren Report
      and Hearings and Exhibits.   Metuchen, N. J.:   Scare-
      crow Press, 1966.
          A valuable tool for researchers since the 26 vol-
      umes of government publications are indexed only by
      name.

599   New York Times, Editors of.   The Witnesses.   New
      York: McGraw-Hill, 1964, 1965.
          A selective compilation of the testimony of wit-
      nesses before the Warren Commission.

600 United States. President's Commission on CIA Activ-
     ities within the United States. Report to the Presi-
     dent by the Commission on CIA Activities within the
     United States. Washington, D. C. : U. S. Government
     Printing Office, 1975.
         Appointed by President Gerald Ford and chaired
     by Vice President Nelson Rockefeller, the Commis-
     sion reported its six-month study. One chapter dealt
     with allegations of CIA involvement in the assassina-
     tion of President Kennedy.

601 United States. President's Commission on the Assas-
     sination of President Kennedy. Investigation of the
     Assassination of President John F. Kennedy. Hear-
     ings ... Pursuant to Executive Order Creating a Com-
     mission to Ascertain, Evaluate, and Report upon the
     Facts Relating to the Assassination of the Late Presi-
     dent, John F. Kennedy and the Subsequent Violent
     Death of the Man Charged with the Assassination.
     Washington, D. C. : United States Government Print-
     ing Office, 1964. 26 vols.
         The complete official record of testimony and
     documents by the Warren Commission. Contains the
     testimony of 552 witnesses and over 3000 documents.

602 United States. President's Commission on the Assas-
     sination of President Kennedy. Report of the Presi-
     dent's Commission on the Assassination of President
     John F. Kennedy. Washington, D. C. : U. S. Govern-
     ment Printing Office, 1964.
         The official edition of the Warren Report sub-
     mitted by the President's Commission. The major
     conclusions were that Lee Harvey Oswald acted as a
     lone assassin and that the Commission found no evi-
     dence supporting a conspiracy, foreign or domestic.

NON-GOVERNMENT PUBLICATIONS
OF THE WARREN COMMISSION REPORT

603 Associated Press. The Warren Report: The Official
     Report on the Assassination of President John F. Ken-
     nedy. New York: Associated Press, 1964.
         The official text with deletions of certain appen-
     dices and photographs. Additional photographs included.

604 Davis, Marc, and Matthews, Jim, eds. Highlights of
     the Warren Report: The Facts and Findings Surround-
     ing the Assassination of John F. Kennedy. Hollywood,
     Calif.: Associated Professional Services, 1964.

605 Doubleday. The Official Warren Commission Report on
     the Assassination of President John F. Kennedy.
     Garden City, N.Y.: Doubleday, 1964.
        Analysis and commentary by attorney Louis Nizer.
     Afterword by historian Bruce Catton.

606 New York Times Co.. Report of the Warren Commis-
     sion on the Assassination of President Kennedy. New
     York: McGraw-Hill, 1963, 1964.
        Contains the entire text of the official report,
     plus an introduction by Harrison Salisbury and four
     related articles by Times reporters.

607 Popular Library. A Concise Compendium of the War-
     ren Commission Report on the Assassination of John
     F. Kennedy. New York: Popular Library, 1964.
        Introduction by Robert J. Donovan.

ADVOCATES OF THE WARREN COMMISSION REPORT

608 Belin, David W. November 22, 1963: You Are the
     Jury. New York: Quadrangle, 1973.
        A book supportive of the Warren Commission Re-
     port written by a counsel to the Commission. Pre-
     sents evidence from testimony of witnesses and docu-
     ments. Rebuts the arguments of some critics.

609 Goldberg, Arthur. Conspiracy Interpretations of the
     Assassination of President Kennedy: International
     and Domestic. Los Angeles: University of California
     Security Studies Project, 1968. (Securities Studies
     Paper no. 16.)
        Summarizes and rebuts several conspiratorial
     theories. The author was a staff member of the War-
     ren Commission and an Air Force historian.

610 Lewis, Richard Warren, and Schiller, Lawrence. The
     Endless Paradox: The Scavengers and Critics of the
     Warren Report. New York: Delacorte, 1967.

A positive appraisal of the Warren Commission
Report and an analysis of several critics. Written by
two journalists who covered the investigation.

Newman, Albert H. The Assassination of John F. Kennedy. (See item 656.)

611 Roberts, Charles. The Truth about the Assassination.
New York: Grosset & Dunlap, 1967.
The author examines several controversial questions pertaining to the assassination. Roberts, a
former crime reporter, was Newsweek's White House
correspondent during Kennedy's administration.

612 Sparrow, John. After the Assassination: A Positive
Appraisal of the Warren Report. New York: Chil-
mark, 1967.
A critique of several early books criticizing the
Warren Report by a noted Oxford scholar.

613 White, Stephen. Should We Now Believe the Warren
Report? New York: Macmillan, 1968.
A book supportive of the Commission's findings
based on four C. B. S. documentaries. The volume is
an expansion of the televised programs.

CRITICISMS AND ALTERNATIVE THEORIES

GENERAL WORKS

614 Anson, Robert Sam. "They've Killed the President!":
The Search for the Murderers of John F. Kennedy.
New York: Bantam, 1975.
A critique of the Warren Commission asserting
a conspiracy and a cover-up of evidence by the C. I. A.
and the F. B. I.

615 Ashman, Charles. The CIA-Mafia Link. New York:
Manor Books, 1975.
An examination of the possible relationship be-
tween the CIA and the Mafia in the assassinations of
John and Robert Kennedy, Sam Giancana, Patrice Lu-
mumba, Rafael Trujillo, and others.

616   Bane, Bernard M.   The Bane in Kennedy's Existence.
      Boston: BMB Pub. Co., 1967.
      An interpretation of the Kennedy assassination as
      a hoax, asserting that the President is still alive.
      Authored by a self-acknowledged former mental pa-
      tient, who in some convoluted way was part of the
      conspiracy.

617   Bane, Bernard M.   Is President Kennedy Alive ... and
      Well? Boston: BMB Pub. Co., 1973.
      A sequel to The Bane in Kennedy's Existence
      (item 616), further extolling the assassination as a
      hoax.

618   Bealle, Morris A.   Guns of the Regressive Right: The
      Only Reconstruction of the Kennedy Assassination That
      Makes Sense.   Washington, D.C.:   Columbia, 1964.

619   Blumenthal, Sid, and Yazijian, Harvey, eds.   Govern-
      ment by Gunplay: Assassination Conspiracy Theories
      from Dallas to Today.   New York: New American
      Library, 1976.
      A collection of 14 articles dealing with assassina-
      tions and crimes in government.

620   Bringuier, Carlos.   Red Friday: November 22nd, 1963.
      Chicago: Charles Hallberg, 1969.
      The author's analysis of the assassination.

621   Buchanan, Thomas G.   Who Killed Kennedy?   New
      York: Putnam, 1964.
      One of the first critical accounts of the Warren
      Commission.   Presents a thesis of right-wing oil in-
      terests conspiring to assassinate the President.

622   Canfield, Michael, and Weberman, Alan J.   Coup d'état
      in America: The CIA and the Assassination of John
      F. Kennedy.   New York: Third Press, 1975.
      Presents documentation indicating the Kennedy
      assassination resulted from a CIA-backed coup d'état.

623   Chapman, Gil, and Chapman, Ann.   Was Oswald Alone?
      San Diego, Calif.: Publishers Export Co., 1967.
      An account of the assassination emphasizing omis-
      sions in the Warren Report and the fact that Tippit
      was murdered two blocks from Ruby's apartment.

624 Cutler, Robert B.   The Flight of CE399:   Evidence of
     a Conspiracy.   Beverly, Mass.:   Printed by Omni-
     Print, 1969.
          An architect's analysis of the flight of the bullet
     which allegedly caused President Kennedy's throat
     wound and Governor Connally's wounds.

625 Cutler, Robert B.   Two Flightpaths: Evidence of Con-
     spiracy.   Danvers, Mass.:   Mirror Press, 1971.
          An analysis with charts and drawings of CE399
     and the "traverse thoracical" bullets and the sixth-
     floor windows of the Texas School Book Depository.

626 David, Jay, ed.   The Weight of the Evidence: The
     Warren Report and Its Critics.   New York: Meredith,
     1968.
          A selection of readings on the assassination both
     pro and con.   Authored by Bill Adler using a pseudo-
     nym.

627 Epstein, Edward Jay.   Inquest: The Warren Commis-
     sion and the Establishment of Truth.   New York:
     Viking, 1966.
          A critical study of the methods and functions of
     the Warren Commission.   Based largely upon inter-
     views with staff members of the Warren Commission.

628 Fox, Sylvan.   The Unanswered Questions about Presi-
     dent Kennedy's Assassination, rev. ed.   New York:
     Award Books, 1965, 1975.
          An expression of doubts about some of the find-
     ings and methods of the Warren Commission by a
     Pulitzer prize-winning journalist.

629 Gershenson, Alvin H.   Kennedy and Big Business.
     Beverly Hills, Calif.:   Book Company of America,
     1964.
          Theorizes that big business assassinated the Pres-
     ident with a long-term and highly complex conspira-
     torial plot.

630 Hanson, William H.   The Shooting of John F. Kennedy;
     One Assassin: Three Shots, Three Hits, No Misses.
     San Antonio, Tex.:   Naylor, 1969.
          A reconstruction at variance with the Warren Re-
     port based on ballistics and investigatory work by the
     author, a retired U. S. A. F. colonel.

631   Hepburn, James. Farewell America. Vaduz, Liechten-
      stein: Frontiers Co., 1968.
      Attributes the assassination to ultra right-wing
      forces, principally Texas oil interests; allegedly is
      based on material foreign intelligence files.

632   Houts, Marshall. Where Death Delights: The Medical
      Story of Dr. Milton Helpbern and Forensic Medicine.
      New York: Coward-McCann, 1967.
      A biography of the chief medical examiner for the
      city of New York. Contains a critique of the autopsy
      procedures and interpretations in the Kennedy investi-
      gation.

633   Joesten, Joachim. The Case Against Lyndon B. John-
      son in the Assassination of President Kennedy. Mu-
      nich: Selbstverlag, 1968-69. 2 vols.
      A speculative account of Johnson's role in the
      assassination.

634   Joesten, Joachim. The Case Against the Kennedy Clan.
      Munich: Selbstverlag, 1967.
      A book based on speculation and rumors.

635   Joesten, Joachim. The Dark Side of Lyndon Baines
      Johnson. London: Dawnay, 1968.
      A negative appraisal of Johnson's Texas background
      and career with implications of his involvement in the
      Kennedy assassination.

636   Joesten, Joachim. How Kennedy Was Killed: The Full
      Appalling Story. London: Dawnay, 1968.
      A summary account from previously published
      books.

637   Joesten, Joachim. Oswald: Assassin or Fall Guy?
      New York: Marzani & Munsell, 1964.
      Postulates the theory that Oswald was used as a
      patsy by a conspiratorial group.

638   Jones, Penn, Jr. Forgive My Grief: A Critical Re-
      view of the Warren Commission Report on the Assas-
      sination of President John F. Kennedy. Volume I.
      Midlothian, Tex.: Midlothian Mirror, 1966.
      Presents a conspiracy theory premised on a vast
      number of deaths of persons related to the assassina-
      tion of President Kennedy and the murders of Oswald
      and Tippit.

639 Jones, Penn, Jr. Forgive My Grief: A Further Crit-
     ical Review of the Warren Commission Report on the
     Assassination of President John F. Kennedy. Volume
     II. Midlothian, Tex. : Midlothian Mirror, 1967.
     Extends the list of mysterious deaths reported in
     vol. I and editorializes on the fraudulent nature of the
     Warren Report's interpretation of ballistics and for-
     ensic evidence.

640 Jones, Penn, Jr. Forgive My Grief.... Volume III.
     Midlothian, Tex. : Midlothian Mirror, 1969.
     Contends the forces behind the Kennedy assassina-
     tion were President Lyndon B. Johnson, the military,
     and independent oil interests.

641 Jones, Penn, Jr. Forgive My Grief: A Further Crit-
     ical Review of the Warren Commission Report on the
     Assassination of President John F. Kennedy. Volume
     IV. Midlothian, Tex. : Midlothian Mirror, 1974.
     A compilation of approximately 100 editorials pub-
     lished from 1970-1974 by the author.

642 Lane, Mark. A Citizen's Dissent: Mark Lane Replies.
     New York: Holt, Rinehart & Winston, 1968.
     A sequel to Rush to Judgment (item 643) in which
     Lane defends his investigation of the assassination and
     describes the attempts to hinder his work by various
     government officials and agencies.

643 Lane, Mark. Rush to Judgment: A Critique of the
     Warren Commission's Inquiry into the Murders of
     President John F. Kennedy, Officer J. D. Tippit,
     and Lee Harvey Oswald. New York: Holt, Rinehart
     & Winston, 1966.
     A negative appraisal of the Warren Commission
     Report by a New York attorney, based in part on inde-
     pendent investigation. (See sequel, item 642.)

644 Lawrence, Lincoln. Were We Controlled? New Hyde
     Park, N. Y. : University Books, 1967.
     An examination of the rumor that Oswald was
     "programmed" to assassinate President Kennedy.

645 McDonald, Hugh C. , and Bocca, Geoffrey. Appointment
     in Dallas: The Final Solution to the Assassination of
     JFK. New York: Hugh McDonald Pub. Co. , 1975.
     A reconstruction of the Kennedy assassination in

which McDonald asserts that a professional assassin,
whom he claims to have traced and interviewed, was
active.

646 MacFarlane, Ian C. Proof of Conspiracy in the Assassination of President Kennedy; Plus 1975 Anthology
and Resources Directory. Melbourne: Book Dis-
tributors, 1975.
Limited edition. Includes a seven-page bibliography.

647 Marcus, Raymond. The Bastard Bullet: A Search for
Legitimacy for Commission Exhibit 399. Los Angeles:
Rendell, 1966.
A small book which analyzes the "magic bullet."
The author alleges the bullet was never fired at a hu-
man target and was planted at the hospital.

648 Marks, Stanley J. Coup d'état: November 22, 1963.
Floral Park, N.Y.: Bureau of International Affairs,
1970.
Suggests a conspiracy was responsible for Kennedy's assassination, plotted by industrialists. A
separate Mafia conspiracy planned an assassination of
Governor John B. Connally.

649 Marks, Stanley J. Two Days of Infamy: November 22,
1963, September 28, 1964. Floral Park, N.Y.:
Bureau of International Affairs, 1969.
A strong attack on the Warren Commission and
the presentation of a theory of conspiracy in the assassinations of John F. Kennedy, Robert F. Kennedy,
and Martin Luther King, Jr. September 28, 1964, is
the date the Warren Commission Report was released.

650 Matteo, Pat. This Captive Land. Yonkers, N.Y.:
private printing, 1968.
An esoteric interpretation of the assassination.

651 Meagher, Sylvia. Accessories after the Fact: The War-
ren Commission, the Authorities and the Report. New
York: Bobbs-Merrill, 1968.
A compendium of omissions, misstatements, mis-
interpretations, and suppressions within the Warren
Report.

652 Model, F. Peter, and Groden, Robert J. JFK: The

Case for Conspiracy. New York: Manor Books, 1976.
Groden, a specialist in photo-optical image restoration, after a study of the photographs and films of the assassination, contends shots originated from four sources.

653 Morin, Relman. Assassination: The Death of President John F. Kennedy. New York: New American Library, 1968.

654 Morrow, Robert D. Betrayal. Chicago: Regnery, 1976.
Morrow, an electronics engineer, claims to have participated in a conspiracy with Tippit, Oswald, Ruby, Ferrie, Shaw, and an artist named Kohly. Because Kennedy had squashed a plot to ruin Cuba's economy by flooding the market with fake pesos, the President's assassination was planned.

655 Nash, George; Nash, Patricia; et al. Critical Reactions to the Warren Report. New York: Marzani & Munsell, 1964.

656 Newman, Albert H. The Assassination of John F. Kennedy: The Reasons Why. New York: Potter, 1970.
An investigation and analysis of Oswald's political development and motivations. Differs with the Warren Commission on Oswald's motives, but also concludes Oswald was the assassin.

657 Noyes, Peter. Legacy of Doubt. New York: Pinnacle Books, 1973.
The author, a Los Angeles television newsman, purports a Mafia-backed plan, based in large part on the presence of underworld figure Eugene Hale Brading in Dealy Plaza at the time of the assassination.

658 O'Toole, George. The Assassination Tapes: An Electronic Probe into the Murder of John F. Kennedy and the Dallas Coverup. New York: Penthouse Press, 1975.
Supports Oswald's innocence by use of data from the psychological stress evaluator, an instrument of lie detection based on voice prints.

659 Popkin, Richard. The Second Oswald. New York:

Avon, 1966.
Contends that two men, one impersonating Oswald, actually shot the President while the real Oswald was a diversionary suspect.

660   Ramparts Magazine, Editors of.   In the Shadow of
      Dallas: A Primer on the Assassination of President
      Kennedy.   San Francisco: Ramparts, 1966, 1967.
      Four previously published articles critical of the
      Warren Commission dealing with (1) mounting sus-
      picions of the Warren Report, (2) editorials by Penn
      Jones, Jr. , (3) a letter written by Jack Ruby from
      jail, and (4) a case for three assassins.

661   Reid, Ed.   The Grim Reapers.   Chicago: Regnery,
      1969.
      An account of the Cosa Nostra (Mafia) by an in-
      vestigative reporter who quotes a former associate of
      Carlos Marcello as stating Marcello hired Oswald to
      assassinate the President.

662   Rice, John F.   What Was Back of Kennedy's Murder?
      Murfreesboro, Tenn. :   Sword of the Lord, 1964.
      A speculative account of the President's assassina-
      tion.

663   Roffman, Howard.   Presumed Guilty: Lee Harvey Os-
      wald in the Assassination of President Kennedy.   Cran-
      bury, N. J. :   Associated University Presses, 1975.
      An analysis of evidence asserting Oswald's inno-
      cence.

664   Sauvage, Leo.   The Oswald Affair: An Examination of
      the Contradictions and Omissions of the Warren Re-
      port.   Cleveland: World Pub. , 1966.
      A theory of conspiracy by white racists written
      by a noted French journalist.

665   Smith, William R.   Assassination by Consensus: The
      Story behind the Kennedy Assassination.   Washington,
      D. C. :   L'Avant Garde, 1966.
      Assassination theory based on "behavior en-
      gineering. "

666   Smith, William R.   A Hog Story from the Aftermire of
      the Kennedy Assassination.   Washington, D. C. :
      L'Avant Garde, 1968.

A theory of right-wing conspiracy by men who profited from the stock and hog markets.

667 Sparrow, Gerald. The Great Assassins. London: John Long, 1968.
An anthology of 18 famous assassinations. One chapter offers a critical interpretation of the Kennedy assassination and investigation.

668 Thompson, Josiah. Six Seconds in Dallas: A Micro-Study of the Kennedy Assassination. New York: Bernard Geis, 1967.
A detailed study of the physical evidence in films and photographs. The author concludes three gunmen fired at President Kennedy.

669 Thomson, George C. The Quest for the Truth: A Quizzical Look at the Warren Report; or, How President Kennedy Really Was Assassinated. Glendale, Calif.: G. C. Thomson Engineering Co., 1964.
An esoteric reconstruction of the assassination whereby five people were killed in Dealy Plaza. According to the author both Kennedy and Connally were being impersonated in the motorcade.

670 Warner, Dale G. Who Killed the President? New York: American Press, 1964.
A highly speculative account.

671 Weisberg, Harold. Oswald in New Orleans. New York: Canyon Books, 1967.
An accounting of Lee Harvey Oswald's activities while living in New Orleans.

672 Weisberg, Harold. Photographic Whitewash: Suppressed Kennedy Assassination Pictures. [Whitewash III. -- See items 674-676.] Hyattstown, Md.: Harold Weisberg, 1967.
An accounting of photographic suppression, omission, and misinterpretation by the Warren Commission and the F. B. I.

673 Weisberg, Harold. Post Mortem: JFK Assassination Coverup Smashed. Frederick, Md.: Harold Weisberg, 1975.
A detailed critique of autopsy, medical, and ballistic evidence concluding that Oswald could not have killed the President.

674   Weisberg, Harold.   Whitewash: The Report on the War-
      ren Report.   Hyattstown, Md. :   Harold Weisberg,
      1965.
      Harsh criticisms of the Warren Report based ex-
      clusively on analysis of the Warren Commission pub-
      lications.

675   Weisberg, Harold.   Whitewash II: The F. B. I. -Secret
      Service Cover-Up.   Hyattstown, Md. :   Harold Weis-
      berg, 1966.
      A critique specifying the misuse and misinterpre-
      tation of evidence by government agencies in the in-
      vestigation of the Kennedy assassination.

676   Weisberg, Harold, with legal analysis by Jim Lesar.
      Whitewash IV: Top Secret JFK Assassination Tran-
      script.   Frederick, Md. :   Harold Weisberg, 1975.
      A critical and legal analysis of recently declassi-
      fied material.   A law suit by Weisberg forced the de-
      classification of much of this material.

677   Wyden, Peter.   The Hired Killers.   London: W. H.
      Allen, 1964.
      Case studies, including the JFK assassination.

678   Zwart, Jacques.   Invitation to Hairsplitting: A Hyper-
      critical Investigation into the True Function of the
      Warren Commission and the True Nature of the War-
      ren Report.   Amsterdam: Paris, 1970.
      A small book contending that proof of a conspiracy
      was intentionally written between the lines of the War-
      ren Report by the President's Commission.

                        GARRISON INQUIRY

678a Brener, Milton E.   The Garrison Case: A Study in
      the Abuse of Power.   New York: Potter, 1969.
      An attorney details the events and methods of
      New Orleans District Attorney Jim Garrison in his
      investigation of the assassination plot.

679   Epstein, Edward Jay.   Counterplot.   New York: Vik-
      ing, 1968.
      A critical analysis of the Garrison inquiry.

680   Flammonde, Paris.   The Kennedy Conspiracy: An Un-

commissioned Report on the Jim Garrison Investigation. New York: Meredith Press, 1969.
    A sympathetic view of Garrison's investigation.
Published prior to the Clay Shaw trial.

681 Garrison, Jim. A Heritage of Stone. New York:
     Putnam, 1970.
        Autobiography by the New Orleans Parish district
     attorney, focusing primarily on his inquiry into the
     assassination of President Kennedy.

682 James, Rosemary, and Wardlow, Jack. Plot or Poli-
     tics? The Garrison Case & Its Cast. New Or-
     leans: Pelican, 1967.
        Two New Orleans newspaper reporters' critical
     account of the Garrison investigation with biographical
     sketches on the major participants.

683 Joesten, Joachim. The Garrison Inquiry: Truth &
     Consequences. London: Dawnay, 1967.
        A journalistic account of the investigation sym-
     pathetic to Garrison.

684 Kirkwood, James. American Grotesque: An Account
     of the Clay Shaw-Jim Garrison Affair in the City of
     New Orleans. New York: Simon and Schuster, 1968,
     1970.
        A detailed account of Garrison's trial of Shaw
     with analysis of pre- and post-trial factors.

                LEE HARVEY OSWALD BIOGRAPHY

     Chapman, Gil, and Chapman, Ann. Was Oswald Alone?
     (See item 623.)

685 Ford, Gerald, and Stiles, John R. Portrait of the
     Assassin. New York: Simon and Schuster, 1965.
        A biography of Lee Harvey Oswald by Rep. Ger-
     ald Ford, a member of the Warren Commission.
     Emphasizes family instability.

686 Hartogs, Renatus, and Freeman, Lucy. The Two As-
     sassins. New York: Crowell, 1965.
        Presents psychiatric comparisons and contrasts of
     Lee Harvey Oswald and Jack Ruby. Hartogs conducted
     a psychiatric interview with Oswald when the alleged
     assassin was a young boy in New York.

687 Hastings, Michael. Lee Harvey Oswald: A Far Mean
     Streak of Indepence Brought on by Negleck. Har-
     mondsworth, England: Penguin Books, 1966.
     Drama.

688 Joesten, Joachim. Marina Oswald. London: Dawnay,
     1967.
         A journalist's speculative account of Oswald's
     wife's background, marriage, and activities.

     Joesten, Joachim. Oswald: Assassin or Fall Guy?
     (See item 637.)

689 Joesten, Joachim. Oswald: The Truth. London:
     Dawnay, 1967.
         A review and rebuttal of rumors about Oswald.

690 Oswald, Robert, with Land, Myrick, and Lang, Bar-
     bara. Lee: A Portrait of Lee Harvey Oswald. New
     York: Coward McCann, 1967.
         A biography of Lee H. Oswald by his brother.

     Popkin, Richard. The Second Oswald. (See item 659.)

691 Ringgold, Gene, ed. Assassin: The Lee Harvey Os-
     wald Biography. Hollywood, Calif.: Associated Pro-
     fessional Services, 1964.
         A biography compiled and revised from the tran-
     scripts of the Warren Report.

     Roffman, Howard. Presumed Guilty.... (See item
     663.)

692 Sites, Paul. Lee Harvey Oswald and the American
     Dream. Elizabeth, N. J.: Pageant, 1967.
         A major biography of Oswald. Includes biblio-
     graphic references.

693 Stafford, Jean. A Mother in History. New York:
     Farrar, Straus and Giroux, 1965.
         Biography of Lee Harvey Oswald's mother based
     on interviews with the subject.

694 Thornley, Kerry. Oswald. Chicago: New Classics
     House, 1965.
         An interpretation of Oswald's political beliefs by
     an author who served in the Marine Corps with him.

Weisberg, Harold. Oswald in New Orleans. (See
item 671.)

JACK RUBY BIOGRAPHY

695 Belli, Melvin. Justice in Dallas. London: Elek Books,
     1964.
     A compendium of factors thwarting the fair trial
     of Ruby in Dallas.

696 Belli, Melvin, and Carroll, Maurice C. Dallas Jus-
     tice: The Real Story of Jack Ruby and His Trial.
     New York: McKay, 1964.
     A personal narrative by the chief counsel for Jack
     Ruby in which the author views the city of Dallas as
     a seat of injustice for the Ruby trial.

697 Gertz, Elmer. Moment of Madness: The People vs.
     Jack Ruby. Chicago: Follett, 1968.
     A record of the trial and subsequent legal pro-
     ceedings by one of Ruby's attorneys.

Hartogs, Renatus, and Freeman, Lucy. The Two Assassins. (See item 686.)

698 Kaplan, John, and Waltz, Jon R. The Trial of Jack
     Ruby. New York: Macmillan, 1965.
     A detailed study by two professors of law.

699 Wills, Garry, and Demaris, Ovid. Jack Ruby. New
     York: New American Library, 1968.
     A biography of Jack Ruby based on interviews
     with Ruby, family, acquaintances, employees, and
     attorneys.

Part VI

TRIBUTES UPON KENNEDY'S DEATH

700 Associated Press. The Torch Is Passed: The Asso-
     ciated Press Story of the Death of a President. New
     York: Associated Press, 1964.
         A pictorial and written account of the assassina-
     tion and funeral.

701 Ballot, Paul. Memorial to Greatness. Island Park,
     N. Y. : Aspen Corp. , 1964.

702 Bergquist, Laura, and Tretick, Stanley. A Very Spe-
     cial President. New York: McGraw-Hill, 1965.
         A personal characterization of the President as
     campaigner, chief executive, and family man in photo-
     graphs and text.

703 Bradlee, Benjamin. That Special Grace. Philadelphia:
     Lippincott, 1963-64.
         A personal tribute to the President by a friend,
     neighbor, and national journalist which depicts many
     of Kennedy's personal qualities--wit, style, intellect,
     etc.

704 Campbell, Earl V. Kennedy's Thoughts after He Was
     Shot. Boston, Mass. : Northwoods Press, 1975.
         A limited edition narrative.

705 Duheme, Jacqueline. John F. Kennedy: A Book of
     Paintings. New York: Atheneum, 1967.
         A collection of paintings on the life and death of
     President Kennedy by a young French artist.

706 Fine, William M. , ed. That Day with God. New
     York: McGraw-Hill, 1965.
         A compilation of 64 sermons delivered on Ken-
     nedy's death.

707   Garduno, Joseph A.   Museum for a President ... John
      F. Kennedy. New York: Carleton, 1966.
         Discusses the proposed JFK Museum of California.
      Includes texts of the Inaugural Address and the unde-
      livered Dallas speech.

708   Goldman, Alex J.   John Fitzgerald Kennedy: The World
      Remembers. New York: Fleet, 1968.
         A compilation by country of memorials dedicated
      to President Kennedy.

709   Gronouski, John S.   Address by John A. Gronouski,
      Postmaster General, at the Dedication of the John
      Fitzgerald Kennedy Memorial Stamp, Boston, Mass.,
      May 29, 1964. Washington, D.C.: Post Office De-
      partment, 1964.

710   Kellner, Abraham, ed.   Sunset at Mid-day: A Tribute
      to the Late John Fitzgerald Kennedy. New York:
      K'Das Pub. Co., 1964.

711   Levy, Clifford V., comp.   Twenty-four Personal Eulo-
      gies on the Late President John F. Kennedy 1917-
      1963. San Francisco: 1963.

712   MacFadden-Bartell Corporation.   A John F. Kennedy
      Memorial. New York: MacFadden-Bartell, 1964.
         A biographical portrayal of President Kennedy
      from boyhood to death combining text, photographs,
      sketches, and quotations.

713   Mansfield, Michael J.   John Fitzgerald Kennedy: Eulo-
      gies to the Late President Delivered in the Rotunda of
      the United States Capitol, November 24, 1963 by Mike
      Mansfield, Earl Warren, and John W. McCormack.
      Washington, D.C.: U.S. Government Printing Office,
      1963.
         Eulogies by the Senate Majority Leader, the Chief
      Justice of the United States and the Speaker of the
      House of Representatives.

714   Matthews, James P., ed.   In Memoriam. Los Angeles:
      Matador Magazine, 1964.
         Primarily a photographic memorial album focusing
      on Kennedy's family and the tributes delivered in his
      memory.

715 Mayhew, Aubrey. The World's Tribute to John F. Kennedy in Medallic Art. New York: Morrow, 1966.
An illustrated collection of coins, medals, tokens, and related items honoring President Kennedy. Part I of the book lists U. S. items and Part II represents items by foreign countries.

716 National Broadcasting Company. "That Was the Week That Was": A Tribute to John Fitzgerald Kennedy. New York: N. B. C. , 1964.
An illustrated text based on the BBC telecast by the same title which was rebroadcast in the United States November 24 and 25, 1963.

717 National Student Association. John Fitzgerald Kennedy, A Tribute ... from the Youth of the United States for the Youth of the World. Philadelphia: U. S. National Student Association, 1964.
A 31-page, illustrated book containing addresses by President Kennedy and sermons on his death.

718 Rajski, Raymond B. , comp. and ed. A Nation Grieved: The Kennedy Assassination in Editorial Cartoons. Rutland, Vt. : Tuttle, 1967.
A collection of editorial cartoons on the Kennedy assassination, primarily from United States publications.

719 Salinger, Pierre, and Vanocur, Sander, eds. A Tribute to John F. Kennedy. Chicago: Encyclopedia Britannica, 1964.
A collection of memorial tributes by reporters and editors in the American and foreign press.

720 Schmidt, Sister M. Bernadette. The Trumpet Summons Us ... John F. Kennedy: A Compilation of Editorials, Columns and Poems. New York: Vantage, 1964.

721 Silverman, Al, ed. John F. Kennedy Memorial Album. New York: MacFadden-Bartell, 1964.
An 80-page book recollecting the life and death of the President.

722 Stewart, Charles J. , and Kendall, Bruce, eds. A Man Named John F. Kennedy: Sermons on His Assassination. Glen Rock, N. J. : Paulist Press, 1964.

A collection of sermons on the meaning of the
life and death of President Kennedy.

723   United States Commission for the United Nations.
      Homage to a Friend: A Memorial Tribute by the
      United Nations for President John F. Kennedy.   New
      York: The Commission in cooperation with the United
      Nations Office of Public Information, 1964.
          A collection of the tributes delivered in the United
      Nations on the death of President Kennedy.

724   United States. Congress. Memorial Addresses in the
      Congress of the United States and Tributes in Eulogy
      of John Fitzgerald Kennedy, Late a President of the
      United States. Washington, D.C.: U.S. Government
      Printing Office, 1964.
          A compilation of all the memorial addresses by
      members of the United States Senate and House of
      Representatives.

725   Walsh, William G., ed. Children Write about John F.
      Kennedy. Brownsville, Tex.: Springman-King, 1964.
          A collection of compositions by children on the
      life and death of the President.

726   Whitbourn, John, ed. Runnymede Memorial. Ilford,
      England: Excel Press, 1965.
          An illustrated program including material on:
      John F. Kennedy Memorial Trust, Kennedy Scholar-
      ships, Runnymede and Magna Carta, the Memorial,
      the Queen's Speech, and Tributes.

Part VII

POETRY

727 Berry, Wendell, and Shahn, Ben. November Twenty
Six Nineteen Hundred Sixty Three. New York:
Braziller, 1964.
A poem on the death and burial of President
Kennedy written by Berry and illustrated by Shahn.

728 Chinmoy, Sri. Kennedy: The Universal Heart. San-
turce, Puerto Rico: Aum Press, 1973.
A collection of 21 poems in tribute to President
Kennedy on the tenth anniversary of his death.

729 Cournos, John. The Lost Leader. New York: Twayne,
1964.
Poetry in tribute to the President.

730 Gardner, Francis V. Rest Assured, John Kennedy.
McLean, Va.: Francis V. Gardner, 1973.

731 Geer, Candy. Six White Horses: An Illustrated Poem
About John-John. Ann Arbor, Mich.: Quill, 1964.
A poem about John F. Kennedy, Jr., and the
death of his father written by a 15-year-old Michigan
high school student.

732 Glikes, Edwin A., and Schwaber, Paul, eds. Of Poetry and Power: Poems Occasioned by the Presidency
and by the Death of John F. Kennedy. New York:
Basic Books, 1964.
A collection of 78 poems.

733 Kazan, Molly. Kennedy. New York: Stein and Day,
1963.
A brief verse written by an American playwright.
Read in the "Actors' Church" on the Sunday following
Kennedy's death.

107

734   Klein, Harry Thiele, ed.   President Kennedy Commem-
      orative Anthology.   Los Angeles: Swordsman Press,
      n. d.

735   Marten, Paul.   Kennedy Requiem.   Toronto: Weller,
      1963.
          Poetry occasioned by the death of the President.

736   Nanchant, Frances Grant.   Song of Peace.   Frances-
      town, N. H. :   Golden Quill, 1969.
          A collection of 78 poems chronicalling the life
      and death of President Kennedy.

737   Vilnis, Aija.   The Bearer of the Star Spangled Banner.
      In Memory of President John Fitzgerald Kennedy.
      Translated by Lilija Pavars.   New York: Speller,
      1964.
          Poetic tribute to the President.

Part VIII

FICTION

738 Bourjaily, Vance. The Man Who Knew Kennedy. New
York: Dial, 1967.
A novel based on the Kennedy generation.

739 Condon, Richard. Winter Kills. New York: Dial,
1974.
A novel which parallels the presidential assassination.

740 DiMona, Joseph. Last Man at Arlington. New York:
Arthur Fields, 1973.
A spy thriller based on the assassination of Pres-
ident Kennedy.

741 Freed, Donald, and Lane, Mark. Executive Action.
New York: Dell, 1973.
Fictional account of a conspiratorial plot to as-
sassinate the President. Basis of a movie by the
same title.

742 Freedman, Nancy. Joshua, Son of None. New York:
Delacorte, 1973.
A novel in which the major character is cloned
from President Kennedy and simulates his life.

743 Garson, Barbara. MacBird. New York: Grove, 1966.
A three-act play of political satire in which the
main characters represent Lyndon B. Johnson and the
Kennedy brothers; John, Robert, and Edward.

744 McCarry, Charles. The Tears of Autumn. New York:
Saturday Review/Dutton, 1975.
A political spy novel with a plausible conspira-
torial plot for Kennedy's assassination.

745 O'Donnell, M. K. You Can Hear the Echo. New York:

Simon and Schuster, 1965.
A novel based on the effects of Kennedy's assassination on the members of one Texas family.

746 Rennert, Maggie. A Moment in Camelot. New York:
Geis, 1968.
A novel based on the political scene of life in
Washington during the Kennedy administration.

747 Singer, Loren. The Parallax View. Garden City,
N.Y.: Doubleday, 1970.
A mystery based on the mysterious or "accidental"
deaths of 25 characters who witnessed the assassination in Dallas.

748 Susann, Jacqueline. Dolores. New York: William
Morrow, 1974.
A thinly-disguised, slim volume depicting the life
of the First Lady from the time of the President's
assassination to her second marriage.

749 Thurston, Wesley S. The Trumpets of November.
New York: Geis, 1966.
A fictitious account of President Kennedy's death
by a conspiratorial plot.

Part IX

JUVENILE LITERATURE

750 Cameron, Gail. Rose. New York: Berkley, 1972.
Gr. 10-.

751 Dareff, Hal. Jacqueline Kennedy: A Portrait in Courage. New York: Parents' Magazine Press, 1965.
Gr. 7-.

752 Eldred, Patricia M. Rose Kennedy. Mankato, Me.:
Creative Educational, 1975.
Gr. 3-6.

753 Fedosiuk, Polly Curren. To Light a Torch: The John
F. Kennedy Story. New York: Guild Press, 1966.
Gr. 4-7.

754 Flavius, Brother. In Virtue's Cause: A Story of John
F. Kennedy. Notre, Inc.: Dujarie, 1967.
Gr. 4-7.

755 Frisbee, Lucy P. John F. Kennedy, Young Statesman.
Indianapolis: Bobbs-Merrill, 1964.
Gr. 3-7.

756 Frolick, S. J. Once There Was a President. New
York: Kanrom, 1964.
Gr. 5-.

757 Graves, Charles P. John F. Kennedy. New York:
Dell, 1966.
Gr. 1-7.

758 Graves, Charles P. Robert F. Kennedy; Man Who
Dared to Dream. Champaign, Ill.: Garrard, 1970.
Gr. 4-7.

759 Hanff, Helene. John F. Kennedy: Young Man of Des-

111

tiny. Garden City, N. Y. : Doubleday, 1965.
Gr. 7-.

760 Hawkes, Ann. Rose Kennedy. New York: Putnam,
1975.
Gr. K-4.

761 Hirsch, Phil, ed. The Kennedy War Heroes. New
York: Pyramid, 1962.
Gr. 7-.

762 Hoopes, Roy. What the President Does All Day. New
York: Day, 1962.
Gr. 4-.

763 Hudson, James A. RFK 1925-1968. New York: Scho-
lastic Book Service, 1969.
Gr. 7-.

764 Kelly, Regina Z. John F. Kennedy. Chicago: Follett,
1969.
Gr. 5-.

765 Kennedy, John F. Profiles in Courage. New York:
Harper & Row, 1955. (Young Reader's Edition.)
Gr. 6-.

766 Kurland, Gerald. Assassination of President John F.
Kennedy. Charlotteville, N. Y. : Sam Har Press,
1973. (Events of Our Times Series, no. 10.)
Gr. 7-10.

767 Kurland, Gerald. Assassination of Robert Kennedy.
Charlotteville, N. Y. : Sam Har Press, 1973. (Events
of Our Times Series, no. 2.)
Gr. 7-10.

768 Lee, Bruce. Boy's Life of John F. Kennedy. New
York: Bold Face Books, 1961.
Gr. 5-.

769 Lee, Bruce, JFK: Boyhood to White House. Greenwich, Conn. : Fawcett, 1961.
Gr. 5-.

770 Lee, Bruce. The Life of John F. Kennedy. New
York: Globe Book Co. , 1964.
Gr. 5-.

771 Lent, Henry Bolles. The Peace Corps: Ambassadors
     of Good Will. Philadelphia: Westminster Press,
     1966.
         Gr. 9-.

772 Levine, Israel E. Young Man in the White House:
     John Fitzgerald Kennedy. New York: Messner, 1964.
         Gr. 7-.

773 Lobsenz, Norman M. The Peace Corps. New York:
     Watts, 1968.
         Gr. 9-.

774 McGuire, Edna. The Peace Corps; Kindlers of the
     Spark. New York: Macmillan, 1966.
         Gr. 7-10.

775 Martin, Patricia M. John Fitzgerald Kennedy. New
     York: Putnam, 1964.
         Gr. K-2.

776 Miers, Earl Schenck. The Story of John F. Kennedy.
     New York: Grosset & Dunlap, 1964.
         Gr. 9-.

777 Reidy, John P. The True Story of John F. Kennedy.
     Chicago: Children's Press, 1967.
         Gr. 6-.

778 Reidy, John P., and Richards, Norman. People of
     Destiny: John F. Kennedy. Chicago: Children's
     Press, 1967. (Humanities Series.)
         Gr. 9-.

779 Sammis, Edward R. John Fitzgerald Kennedy, Youngest
     President. New York: Scholastic Book Service, 1961.
         Gr. 9-.

780 Schoor, Gene. Young John Kennedy. New York: Har-
     court, Brace & World, 1963.
         Gr. 7-.

781 Schoor, Gene. Young Robert Kennedy. New York:
     McGraw-Hill, 1969.
         Gr. 7-.

782 Steinberg, Alfred. The Kennedy Brothers. New York:

Putnam, 1969.   (Lives to Remember.)
Gr. 7-11.

783 Stewart, John C. Our Hero, John F. Kennedy. North-
port, Ala.: American Southern Pub. Co., 1964.
Gr. 7-.

784 Strousse, Flora. John Fitzgerald Kennedy: Man of
Courage. New York: Harcourt, Brace & World,
1963.
Gr. 7-.

785 Tregaskis, Richard W. John F. Kennedy and PT-109.
New York: Random House, 1962.
Gr. 7-.

786 Vinton, Iris. Story of President Kennedy. New York:
Grosset & Dunlap, 1966.
Gr. 4-6.

787 Webb, Norbert N. The Living J. F. K. New York:
Grosset & Dunlap, 1964.
Gr. 3-7.

788 White, Nancy. Meet John F. Kennedy. New York:
Random House, 1965.
Gr. 2-5.

789 Wilkens, Frances. President Kennedy. London: Cas-
sell, 1962.
Gr. 7-.

790 Wood, James P. The Life and Words of John F. Kennedy. Elm Grove, Wis.: Country Beautiful Foundation, 1964. (Dist. by Doubleday.)
Gr. 4-.

INDEX OF AUTHORS,
EDITORS, AND COMPILERS

115

INDEX OF TITLES

125